CONVERSATIONAL COMMENTARY ON
ACTS
Gospel Mission Then and Now

BY MICHELLE MYERS

Conversational Commentary on Acts:
Gospel Movement Then and Now

©2022 Myers Cross Training
His Way Resources, Inc.
Design + Layout ©2022 Erica Zoller Creative, LLC

All rights reserved. No part of this publication may be reproduced, distributed, or transmitted in any form or by any means, including photocopying, recording, or other electronic or mechanical methods, without the prior written permission of the publisher, except in the case of brief quotations embodied in critical review and certain other noncommercial uses permitted by copyright law.

ISBN 978-1-7345281-8-3

CONTENTS

Acknowledgments	Page 1
Introducing Conversational Commentary	Pages 3-5
Introduction to Acts	Pages 7-8
CHAPTER 1 Commentary	Pages 11-13
Questions	Page 14
CHAPTER 2 Commentary	Pages 15-18
Questions	Pages 19-20
CHAPTER 3 Commentary	Pages 21-23
Questions	Pages 24-25
CHAPTER 4 Commentary	Pages 26-29
Questions	Pages 30-31
CHAPTER 5 Commentary	Pages 32-35
Questions	Pages 36-37
CHAPTERS 6-7 Commentary	Pages 38-42
Questions	Pages 43-44
CHAPTERS 8-9 Commentary	Pages 45-52
Questions	Pages 53-54

CONTENTS

CHAPTERS 10-11 Commentary   Pages 55-60
Questions   Pages 61-62

CHAPTERS 12-13 Commentary   Pages 63-69
Questions   Pages 70-71

CHAPTERS 14-15 Commentary   Pages 72-78
Questions   Pages 79-80

CHAPTERS 16-17 Commentary   Pages 81-89
Questions   Pages 90-91

CHAPTERS 18-20 Commentary   Pages 92-101
Questions   Pages 102-103

CHAPTERS 21-23 Commentary   Pages 104-109
Questions   Pages 110-111

CHAPTERS 24-26 Commentary   Pages 112-118
Questions   Pages 119-120

CHAPTERS 27-28 Commentary   Pages 121-127
Questions   Pages 128-129

Three Concluding Thoughts   Pages 130-131

Recommended Resources   Page 133

Acknowledgments

My Bible margins are filled with notes I've written over the years -- a combination of sermons heard and books read, lecture notes during seminary, insights from countless discipleship groups, retreats and conferences, as well as my own personal study. To all who have used your gifts as stewards of God's grace, I am forever grateful for your investment in my life and the lives of many others. *James, Noah, Cole + Shea:* I am so glad God gave me you. Thank you for always being my biggest cheerleaders. *Somer, Liz, Erica, Teeny + Kennedi:* thank you for ensuring there was a way for this series to happen. I am so glad God put me on your team! And finally, to the place I get to call home and people I get to call family, I am so grateful to God for Biltmore Church. I love the shared call we have and the work we see God doing as we live the truths inside the book of Acts together in WNC.

SHE WORKS HIS WAY

CONVERSATIONAL COMMENTARY ON ACTS:

Introducing Conversational Commentary

Some of my favorite moments take place in church or a living room with other women gathered around an open Bible. It's during those moments when I see for myself that God's Word is living and active *(Hebrews 4:12)*, when I'm taught by older women and am able to teach younger women, and when that teaching isn't merely done with words but is coupled with an example *(Titus 2:1-5)*.

So when God first began stirring this series in my heart, I wondered if it would be possible to create a gospel-centered conversation that would take place inside gospel community -- not just writing content. Because this world is not lacking in good -- *yes, even gospel-centered* -- information. We also have more distribution channels to provide the information to more people in ways that are quick, cost-efficient, and convenient to access. I'm grateful for these outlets. Any place the gospel can be proclaimed is reason to rejoice. But the good information and great distribution are not enough on their own. As believers, we're *all* called to be disciples who make disciples -- and that cannot be automated and distributed, delegated to some, or designed for the masses.

So that's where the idea of writing conversational commentary began. God's Word is God speaking to us, we get to continue the conversation He started in the commentary, and the corresponding questions enable you to build discipleship relationships with women you know.

WHAT TO EXPECT: GOSPEL-CENTERED CONVERSATION

When I'm doing a deep dive into a particular book, I have between 6-10 resources that I dig into that range from study Bibles and concordances to theological dictionaries and systematic theology books. *(See the back for my reference guide of my favorite Bible study tools. And for reference, throughout this commentary when I quote scripture, I am using the English Standard Version.)* In this series, the goal is to supply enough historical context and theological explanation for deep understanding without crossing over into so much head knowledge that it distracts from the main message of the gospel. Should you come across something "missing" in the commentary, that likely means we felt elaborating on it would divert the conversation into secondary issues that too often divide rather than unify.

There's also a reason we chose to call this *conversational* commentary: because I want you to feel like you're sitting in my living room with a cup of coffee and an open Bible. The verse-by-verse commentary is anchored in truth about God, but His truth also invites us to lovingly respond. I loved the opportunity to include in the commentary how God has moved in my heart to obey the truth in the text.

WHAT TO EXPECT: COMMENTARY BY WOMEN FOR WOMEN

While my being a woman does not change the truth written in God's Word, it does affect my perspective, what obedience practically looks like, and the roles and experiences God has given me in my life. While these conversations and questions could absolutely be used in mixed-gender settings, I wanted to provide commentary and questions that specifically address God's design for women as well as women's roles as partners in the gospel, wives and moms -- among many others. God's Word has shaped how I see every role in my life and every place He has called me. I pray this series equips women to fulfill the Great Commission *(Matthew 28:19-20)* and to see their valuable place in God's work in the world.

WHAT TO EXPECT: MULTIPLICATION THROUGH DISCIPLESHIP

In the last letter he wrote before he was killed, Paul gave Timothy some descriptors of the Lord's servant, one being *"able to teach" (2 Timothy 2:24)*. Paul is not advocating to Timothy that all of God's servants must be skilled communicators, but that they must *know the* truth so they can *teach* the truth to others. Some have long regarded teaching merely as a spiritual gift. And while God has certainly given some the gift of teaching, teaching is more than a gift. Teaching cannot be separated from discipleship. You wouldn't have this book in your hand if you didn't feel called to know God more through His Word. But what you are compelled to *know*, you should also be compelled to *share*.

WHAT TO EXPECT: GROUP DISCUSSION QUESTIONS

Along with commentary for verse-by-verse study, I've included questions for group discussion. I've done my best to follow a formula my husband *(one of the most passionate people about discipleship that I know)* calls *peeling the onion* -- a method where the questions require more thought and transparency the deeper into the discussion you go. Specifically, each discussion begins with an icebreaker that is based on personal experience. Next, there are 2-4 questions with answers that are relatively simple to find right there in the text. Finally, the discussion concludes with another 2-3 questions that require more personal reflection, accountability and application.

If you have a spiritually mature group, you may not need to use the provided questions at all. These open-ended questions could work to guide a great discussion for each meeting:

1. *What stood out to you most? Did you notice anything for the first time?*
2. *What did this text prompt you to pray for/about?*
3. *Based on what you read, what action do you need to take in your life to obey what you learned?*

A note of encouragement: The discussion will get easier as your group meets with more frequency. It's normal for conversation to be quieter in the beginning, so don't be discouraged if it feels like you're doing a lot of the talking when your group is new. Make it your goal to talk less each week and make sure you're waiting long enough after you ask a question before you jump in to answer it yourself. Moments of silence feel longer when you're the one initiating the conversation – so be okay with a few pauses in conversation. Someone will jump in eventually, and the silence gaps will get shorter as your group becomes more comfortable with one another.

As noted at the beginning, though, discipleship is not merely words. Bringing people in closer to you will provide you with opportunities to demonstrate the gospel through your care for them and your actions in general. These moments are not secondary to your time spent teaching. Take the time to love deeply. As my pastor, Bruce Frank, says all the time, "Declare *and* demonstrate the gospel."

Praying for you and your group! May God speak powerfully to us through His Word.

In Him,
Michelle

SHE WORKS HIS WAY

CONVERSATIONAL COMMENTARY ON ACTS:

Introduction to Acts

The book of Acts was written by Luke, who is also the author of the Gospel of Luke, between A.D. 63 and 70. Acts begins right where Luke ends, so the two accounts were probably meant to be read together as a joint work. It's easy to skip over the title of the book, since most New Testament books are either the name of a person or a city. But what we often shorten to Acts stands for the Acts of the Apostles. The entire point of this book is to show the acts or the actions of the apostles as they were led by the Holy Spirit after Jesus ascended into heaven. This book records real events that *actually* happened in history and contains the stories of real people who *actually* lived. This book tells the story of the explosive growth of the early church and the expansion of the gospel. Acts is the bridge between the gospels of Jesus and the Epistles *(Letters)* to the churches that follow.

This is *not* the book of reactions, or of plans, policies, and procedures. Acts stands for progress and movement. The same Holy Spirit that was alive and active then is alive and active now. The same movement that began then is the same movement every believer is still part of now.

As you read, pay close attention to:

The Holy Spirit

It's easy to fall to the extremes of how you view the Holy Spirit. Some view Him as the unspoken Person of the Trinity (my friend Jeannie Cunnion coined the phrase *"weird uncle of the Trinity"*) or the "for show" aspect of the worship service. Neither is accurate. The Holy Spirit is neither to be ignored or exploited.

Remember these words of Jesus: *"Nevertheless, I tell you the truth: it is to your advantage that I go away, for if I do not go away, the Helper [the Holy Spirit] will not come to you. But if I go, I will send Him to you"* (John 16:7).

Jesus Himself was the one who told us that it would be better for us to have the Holy Spirit inside us than to have Him beside us. So let the book of Acts help form your thoughts of who the Holy Spirit is, not merely what you may have or have not experienced.

Miracles

The apostles perform many wonders and signs, just as Jesus did. But there is a pattern and a possible bigger picture on display between the person and the miracle:

1) Only unbelievers are healed. *(Your greatest pain may be the pathway to Jesus.)*
2) Only believers are raised from the dead. *(In Christ, life isn't over for us.)*

Growth

Luke cataloged how God grew the early church. The Holy Spirit prompted, the disciples and believers obeyed, and the world around them paid attention. Many were saved. We have been given the same charge and the same assignment. *How are you active in this movement?*

Joy

Believers rejoice in the book of Acts for two reasons:

1. **Salvation:** In the face of both persecution or rejection, the gospel is still being shared, and people are being saved. It doesn't matter if they get run out of town, stoned or imprisoned, there is great rejoicing when people get saved.

2. **Suffering:** Because they had watched Jesus suffer for the gospel, they rejoiced in suffering because they saw it as confirmation they were continuing the work Jesus had done.

Acts 1

COMMENTARY

1:1 The "first book" mentioned here is the gospel of Luke. *Theophilus* means "lover of God," so it could have been written to a specific person, but more than likely, Luke was writing to all those who love God.

In Greek sentence structure, words are listed in order of importance. Note that *"do"* is mentioned before *"teach."* Luke emphasized the importance of what Jesus *did* before referencing what Jesus *taught*. The same sentiment is true for us. We should prioritize the way we live for God over merely what we teach others about Him.

1:2-3 Jesus started the gospel movement that we are a part of today. He began building His church, and He still gives us the same gracious power through the Holy Spirit. The "many proofs" that he showed to the apostles were to strengthen their faith to continue the work.

1:4-5 Jesus instructed them to wait for the Holy Spirit before scattering to share the gospel. We often distinguish waiting from the work, but sometimes, waiting *is* the work. The word Spirit, referring to the Holy Spirit, occurs 70 times in the book of Acts – more than all of the gospels combined.

1:6-8 We'd love to know the *how* and *when* of God's every move, but that's simply unnecessary. Simply trusting His timing and His ways increase our faith instead of merely increasing our knowledge. Look how Jesus answers their question. Instead of explicitly answering the question they asked, He reminds them of who God is and the work they should do. When we find ourselves asking God a specific question, we can remind ourselves of the same truths while we wait on His timing.

1:8   All believers have access to the same Holy Spirit. There's no such thing as half Holy Spirit for new believers or Holy Spirit Jr. for kids. The Holy Spirit is a believer's power source, and as noted here, the Holy Spirit's power will lead you to spotlight the work of Jesus as His witness.

Also, please note that your "Jerusalem" is the city where you live, your *"Judea"* includes your surrounding areas, and *"to the ends of the earth"* includes every place you go. Keep increasing your circle of where you take Christ and go in this order. Confession: it's often easier to go on a short-term mission trip and live sold out for Jesus and return home to a regular routine of living for yourself. This world is not our home, and your primary mission field is where God has you go daily: your neighborhood, your community, your workplace, your kid's school, the gym, the local coffee shop, etc. Live on mission.

1:9   Going back to Exodus and the Israelites in the wilderness, a cloud is synonymous with God's presence.

1:11   We wait with expectation for Christ's return, not by staring into the heavens, but by doing His work and being His witnesses. When Jesus returns, we will not miss it! Just as He ascended boldly and visibly, He will return in the same way.

1:12   A "Sabbath day's journey" was about 0.6 miles. This was the maximum distance that could be traveled without being considered work.

1:14   Jesus told them to wait for the Holy Spirit, so prayer was the main activity while they waited. If you are waiting, that doesn't mean you can't do anything. You can pray while you wait.

1:15-18   In front of the 120 people who were gathered and waiting for the Holy Spirit, Peter noted they needed to replace Judas as an apostle. *(And yes, these are the gory details of what happened to Judas. Yikes!)*

1:20   Cross-reference to Psalm 69:25.

1:20-23   Of the 120 gathered, two met the requirements for apostleship: a man who had accompanied the apostles from the baptism of

John until Jesus' ascension back into heaven. Note that women were in the room *(vs. 14 lists the women and Mary)*. The women were not eligible for the office or title of apostle, but they were included in the work. Not having a title does not mean exclusion. Women were included in Jesus' ministry, and women were very much part of the early church.

1:24 They began prayerfully deciding between the two men (Joseph and Matthias). All decisions you make should start with prayer.

1:25 The language used (*"take the place in this ministry"*) shows replacing Judas wasn't about merely replacing him by title or task. Kingdom work is always primarily about the ministry being done, not the one doing it.

1:26 Apostle and disciple are often used interchangeably. *Disciple* means follower/learner. *Apostle* means messenger/missionary.

Acts 1

QUESTIONS

Icebreaker: The disciples had to have felt helpless and in over their head after Jesus called them to continue the work He started until His return. Has there ever been a time in your life when you felt that way – like the job you'd been given was too hard to do on your own? Tell us about it.

1. What does Jesus do for the 40 days He is with His followers after His resurrection?

2. What do they ask Jesus in 1:6? Why do you think this is the question they have for Him? What does Jesus say in response, and what can we learn from His response?

3. Acts 1:8 is really the primary directive for the apostles then and for us now. Read this verse again, and then answer the following questions: What are they called to do? Where should they do it? How will they be able to do it?

4. Define and write down your Jerusalem (where you live), your Judea (your surrounding areas), and your ends of the earth (everywhere you go). Where do you find yourself most active in the mission of God, and where do you currently go where you have previously not considered the primary reason you're there is to be His witness?

5. What words would you use to describe your role as His witness? What needs to change in your heart and life for Jesus to be able to advance His Kingdom through you?

6. As a group, brainstorm what it would look like for Acts 1:8 to be alive and evident in your group or church. Rewrite Acts 1:8 in your own words as your group's mission statement. (Tip: Make it easy to memorize!)

7. What was the main activity of the disciples while they waited for the Holy Spirit? Do you find yourself drawn to prayer while you wait? Why or why not?

Close: Pray over the mission statement you created as a group and ask God to continuously convict you to make that statement a reality.

Acts 2

COMMENTARY

2:1 The miraculous moment in the verses that follow (that we now call Pentecost) was set up by simple obedience to stay together and wait for the Holy Spirit. Don't neglect simple obedience. Simple obedience is the setup for God to do a miracle.

2:2 In Scripture, wind represents the spirit or creative breath of God. This was a sign that God was about to accomplish a work of renewal. The eyewitnesses of Jesus were experiencing the presence of God and being empowered for the following prophetic ministry.

2:3 *"Divided tongues of fire"* refers to both power and purity. Since fire purifies and is powerful, a fire was often associated with God's presence in the Old Testament.

2:4-11 The gift of tongues is often misunderstood and not frequently mentioned, but here are the three things we know about tongues from this passage: 1) Every syllable is entirely guided by the Holy Spirit *(vs. 4)*; 2) Tongues will be understood by someone else there *(vs. 6-8)* and 3) Tongues will declare the mighty works of God *(vs. 11)*.

2:12-13 Some were amazed by the gift of tongues and others joked they must be drunk. The same will be true for you. Some will be amazed by what you do under the direction of the Holy Spirit, and others will mock you. Do not be surprised or delayed by others' misunderstanding of what the Holy Spirit prompts you to say and do. You can expect opposition to what you do on God's behalf.

2:14-15 You can choose to see others' misunderstanding as criticism, or as Peter did, you can choose to see it as curiosity and offer an explanation. Peter's sermon was prompted by the mocking he received from some.

2:16-21 Cross-reference to Joel 2:28-32.

2:22-24 Everything that happened to Jesus – from the works and miracles He performed to His crucifixion – was fully and completely under God's control.

2:25-28 Cross-reference to Psalm 16:8-11

2:25-36 Peter realizes that they do not believe in Jesus, but he knows they believe the writing of King David. Here, Peter uses the former Israelite king's words to show how David spoke of His salvation and how Jesus would conquer death.

2:33 This one verse shows the distinction and roles of the Trinity or Triune God – God the Father, Jesus the Son, and the Holy Spirit. God promised the Holy Spirit *(that Peter referenced from the prophet Joel)*, then Christ was seated at the right hand of God when His work on earth was accomplished and received authority from God the Father to send the Holy Spirit in a powerful way at Pentecost.

2:34-35 Cross-reference to Psalm 110:1.

2:36 Although Jesus was called Lord and Messiah previously, the full authority of these titles is only granted through the death, resurrection, and exaltation. Peter's proclamation indicates that something has changed. Through Jesus, salvation is now available to the world.

2:37-38 Repentance means a *change in direction* – not merely remorse. So when those who wish to be saved ask what to do, Peter tells them to change the direction of their lives and follow Jesus. Salvation is given by God through faith in Jesus, and baptism is both an outward expression and public declaration of the change that occurred on the inside.

2:39 By listing all who the promise is for, Peter reiterates that salvation is a free gift that is available to all who believe.

2:41 Always remember that people are not numbers; they are souls.

2:42-47 This is a beautiful picture of genuine Biblical community. These verses describe what the local church looked like when it started, and it's what it should look like now. I encourage you to write the name of your church here in the margin of your Bible. As you read this passage, before allowing yourself to say, *"My church doesn't look like that,"* examine yourself first. Does *your life* look like this? Deep community starts small and grows from there. If it doesn't currently exist in your church, let it begin with you.

2:42 They were devoted to 1) the apostles teaching, 2) to the fellowship, 3) to the breaking of bread, and 4) to prayer. Devotion implies they were all in, not half-committed. We can't expect the rich community described here if we only have half-hearted commitment. Being devoted to the apostles' teaching reminded them of what brought them together: the gospel. The gospel saves you once, but it's also what sustains you as a believer, so we must stay devoted to the teaching of the gospel. But just as it would be strange to have a church that didn't ever teach the gospel, it should be just as strange to go into a building once a week to listen to teaching but not know the people worshiping with you. Devotion was not merely to the apostles teaching, but also to the fellowship. Don't just attend church and check the box. Invest in relationships there. Have meals together. Pray together. Community matters!

2:43-44 *"Having all things in common"* didn't mean they all agreed on everything. But because they kept the gospel and their beliefs at the center of their gatherings, they could stay unified because the gospel was ultimate, and everything else could be secondary. Whenever believers lose their unity, something has become more important than Jesus. So stay unified around what matters most, and don't divide with fellow believers over lesser things.

2:45 This is not merely describing giving out of the abundance but giving out of their current possessions. What could prompt such mind-blowing generosity? Love. Think about it: it's not hard to give someone you love something they need. Generosity only becomes problematic in the absence of love. If generosity is a struggle for you, what can you do to deepen your love for those around you? *[Hint: you can't muster it up on your own. Let God fill you with His love, so you can overflow with His love to others.]*

2:46 Biblical community occurs here in two places: in the temple and in homes. Both are mentioned not because both are options

– but because opening and gathering in both locations are necessary. People tend to gravitate to extremes on this, either only having gospel community inside the church building or believing the only gospel community they need can happen inside their home. Pursue gospel community in both places: inside the church and inside homes.

2:46-47 Thriving gospel community will be marked by joy, generosity, worship, and salvations. Aim for these marks; aiming for anything else will be a distraction.

2:47 God gives growth and changes hearts. He saves. He will add to your numbers, so you do not have to strategize for growth. Cultivate the activity laid out in the previous verses, and trust God to do His job. He is mighty to save!

Acts 2

QUESTIONS

Icebreaker: Describe a time in your life when you either witnessed or experienced incredible unity. When was it, and what was it like?

1. What were the disciples doing when the Holy Spirit came? Do you think it matters that their simple obedience prompted a miracle? Do you think we ever expect a miracle without being willing to obey in the simple acts? How do we train ourselves to see obedience as our role in the miracles God can still do today?

2. What were the two different reactions of those who witnessed the believers speaking in tongues? Do you think some will always misunderstand what God calls us to say and do? Should the way others respond to God's call on our lives affect our boldness and obedience?

3. Read Acts 2:14. Peter preached the sermon, but who stood with him? How do you stand with those who are called to preach and teach? Or if you are the one teaching, who is standing with you? Do you think we would be bolder for Christ if we came together more? How can you partner together more with other believers and increase your boldness?

4. In Peter's sermon, he showed how Joel prophesied about the coming of the Holy Spirit and how David's writings pointed to Jesus as the Messiah. Many in the crowds were convinced and asked what they should do. Read Acts 2:38-39 for Peter's response to their question. What does repentance mean? Who is salvation available for? What is required for salvation? What is the symbolism of baptism?

5. Have a group member read Acts 2:42-47 aloud again. What words and phrases stand out to you as you read? Why?

6. Acts 2:42 lists four things that had the believer's devotion. What were the four things? What does it mean to be devoted? Do you think we ever give Christ half-hearted effort while expecting all-in results? How would you describe the difference between devotion and half-commitment? How can we stay accountable to full devotion?

7. The early church prioritized a good mix of theological activity (such as prayer and teaching) with relational activity (such as breaking of bread, meeting in homes, sharing with one another as they had needs, etc.). Do you think it would increase our unity as a local church/group if we prioritized both theological and relational activity? Which one is easier for you, and which one do you need to make more effort to prioritize? What's one action you can take this week in the area where you are weakest?

Close: Work together to re-word Acts 2:42-47 into a written prayer you can pray over your group and over your local church. Have each group member copy it down and pray it over your group every day this week.

Acts 3

COMMENTARY

3:1 This was an ordinary day. Peter and John were going to the temple at the hour of prayer as they did each day. Of course, a miracle will occur, but the miracle wasn't the point or the goal. They were simply practicing ordinary obedience.

3:2 There are so many little notes about the importance of community threaded throughout the entire book of Acts. Even here, we see that the man about to be healed had to be carried (by family and/or friends) to beg at the temple daily. In a world that is only increasing in autonomy, recognize the importance of community.

Alms means "money or goods."

3:3-5 People may expect to get something from you, but they do not expect to get something from God. Like Peter and John, be willing to be the bridge that helps others get to God. Through the power of the Holy Spirit, God uses His people to do His work.

3:4 Peter and John looked at the man who was in need. Between looking down at our phones or simply avoiding eye contact with those we encounter as we go throughout our day, we may miss opportunities to minister simply because we don't lock eyes with those we meet. You may be amazed how many more opportunities God gives you to meet the needs of others just by being willing to look up.

3:6-7 First, note the power came from Jesus, not Peter. But also, notice how Peter extended his faith to the lame man. Just imagine how scary it would have been to be told to get up and walk when you had been lame from birth. Instead, Peter had confidence in the power of God to heal the man, so he took the man by the hand and raised him up so he could see that he had been healed.

3:7-8   Note the progression of the man's faith. He stood, began to walk, and finally, he entered the temple, leaping and praising God.

3:9-12 Curiosity is created when God moves like He moved to heal the lame man. Follow His movements with praise and an explanation. Words and actions work together as our witness. When Peter saw the people were amazed, he offered an explanation for the man's healing by sharing about Jesus.

3:12-26 This is Peter's 2nd sermon in the book of Acts, and once again, because he is speaking to a Jewish audience, he continues to show how Jesus was the promised Messiah who fulfilled all the prophecy in the Old Testament.

3:13-15 Peter does not hold back. He reminds them *(and us!)* of exactly what they have to repent for: they delivered Jesus over, denied Him as God's Son, and had Him killed – even though Jesus is the One who gives them life.

3:16   *"Name"* refers to everything that is true about a person in a Biblical sense. So by reminding them that this man healed in the name of Jesus, he was declaring that Jesus was the Son of God. Jesus even gave Peter the faith in Him to heal the lame man. The proof of Christ's identity was in the miracle they had just witnessed.

3:17-19 Peter empathizes that they did not know Jesus was the Christ when they killed Him, but he also doesn't hold back that ignorance doesn't free us from responsibility. Repentance is still necessary.

3:19   The beauty of the phrase *"turn back"* is a beautiful picture of reminding us that God created us, so we all start with Him. The call of repentance to turn back to Him shows both His power to save and the reminder of His love that He initiated with us from the beginning.

3:19-20 Repentance often has a negative connotation, as most of us don't love to admit when we are wrong. But look at what repentance brings: when we repent of our sin and confess Christ as Lord, our sins are blotted out, the presence of the Lord refreshes us, and we have the assurance that Christ will return for us. So rush to repent - don't delay! Repentance is a beautiful gift that should drive us to run toward God with gratitude instead of running from God in shame.

3:21-25 Peter mentions all the Old Testament prophets collectively, and he selectively mentions Moses *(quoting Deuteronomy 18:15)*, Samuel, and Abraham *(quoting Genesis 12:3)*. Given that not much time has passed since Christ's crucifixion, Peter's boldness in declaring Jesus as the fulfillment of these prophets was true, but was not a popular message and was bound to receive backlash. Truth and popularity will not always align.

Acts 3

QUESTIONS

Icebreaker: Have you ever witnessed God do an incredible miracle? Something that could not be explained by human logic? What effect did witnessing that miracle have on your faith?

1. Once again, look how the miracle occurred out of ordinary obedience. They didn't plan to heal a lame man. They just showed up in ordinary obedience. What are areas of your life that require your ordinary obedience? Do you ever act or expect God to do a miracle there? Why or why not?

2. The man was a beggar, so he expected to get something from Peter and John, but he didn't expect to get something from God. When we encounter people who have needs, what would it look like to give them something from God instead of just giving them something from us?

3. It seems strange that we live in a world where this needs to be pointed out, but Peter and John were able to heal the man because they looked at him first. Do you really look at people who are around you? Do you ever miss opportunities to minister to others just because you're not looking others in the eyes? What distracts you or deters you from noticing those around you?

4. The people were in amazement when they saw the lame man leaping and praising God, so Peter took the opportunity to offer an explanation for the miracle. What do you think you lean on more often to witness to others - words or actions? Why? Since both matter, how do you think you could grow in the area where you are less comfortable?

5. The phrase "turn back" in vs. 19 reminds us that God created us, so we all start with Him. Is it hard for you to believe that God loved you first? Why or why not?

6. Have a group member read Acts 3:19-20 aloud. What three things do these verses remind us that repentance makes possible? Since these promises are so incredible, why do you think we often run from God in shame instead of running to God in repentance?

7. The same power of the Holy Spirit that healed the lame man is the power that gave Peter the boldness to preach a truthful but unpopular message. Both times it wasn't Peter, but it was the Holy Spirit's power through Peter. How do you think we could live more in the power of the Holy Spirit and less in our own strength?

Acts 4

COMMENTARY

4:1 The captain of the temple was second in command after the high priest.

4:2 The Sadducees did not believe in the resurrection *(Luke 20:27)*, so that's why they were "greatly annoyed" by Peter and John's preaching. Believing in the death and resurrection of Christ is vital for every believer because 1) it's proof that everything Jesus said and did was true *(as well as all of the Old Testament prophets)*; 2) Jesus' death satisfied the payment for our sins and makes salvation possible; 3) In the resurrection, Jesus conquered death, and in Him, we will too and spend eternity with Him in heaven. *[For a deeper study on the importance of the resurrection, dig into 1 Corinthians 15.]*

4:2-4 Always stay focused on the Kingdom result, not your success or circumstances. The disciples were arrested, but thousands of people were saved!

4:8 Pay attention to how many times you find the phrase *"filled by the Holy Spirit"* as you read through Acts. Luke attributes the boldness of Peter's actions to the power of the Holy Spirit, and we should do the same. Make efforts to not grow numb to the power of the Holy Spirit and refuse to take credit for the Holy Spirit's work in our lives.

4:9-11 Peter's gospel presentation has three main points. He begins with 1) the fact of the miracle with evidence, then moves to 2) man's role in Jesus' death, and finally 3) an invitation to accept Jesus' gift of salvation.

4:9 Peter once again points to the evidence of Christ's power through the miracle of the lame man's healing. Remember that the faith we have as believers hinges on real events! Jesus *really* came to earth, *really* died on the cross, and *really* rose from the grave after three days. When you share your faith, you're not merely sharing a theological opinion, but you're sharing about *real* events that *really* happened! Everyone may not agree with who Jesus was or how the tomb was empty, but secular history reports all agree that Jesus really lived, really died, and that the tomb *was* empty.

4:11 At that time, a cornerstone was the most important stone in a building's foundation. Cross-reference to Psalm 118:22 and Isaiah 28:16.

4:12 Christ's salvation is both exclusive and inclusive. It's exclusive in that salvation is found *only* through faith in Jesus, but it's inclusive in that His salvation is available to *all*.

4:13 The leaders of the Sanhedrin were astonished at their boldness because they recognized Peter and John had been with Jesus. There will be a difference in your behavior when you have been with Jesus, not just when you know about Jesus. People will notice when you have been with Jesus.

4:14-16 A changed life is a powerful testimony. People can argue about theology and opinions, but it's hard to argue against a changed life. If you want to live for Christ, aim to live changed.

4:16-17 The leaders couldn't argue with the testimony in front of them, but they chose to act out of fear of people and a desire to keep their own power and influence. When you make decisions, go deeper than merely examining your actions. Examine your motives. Consider what guides how you make decisions. Aim for fear of God, not fear of man, and have faith in God's power over working to secure your own influence.

4:19-21 Don't forget that not long ago, these men were hiding and denying that they were Jesus' disciples. Now, they are boldly confessing Christ in the face of persecution and opposition. The difference? The power of the Holy Spirit. That same power is available to all believers.

Also, note that there are varying opinions on the role government and governing officials should play in our lives. Here, we see

Peter and John defying the government's requests, which some would say either disproves or disobeys the command to submit to governing authorities in Romans 13. It's important to note that the government officials were asking Peter and John to no longer speak in the name of Jesus, which directly would disobey Jesus' commandment to be His witnesses *(Acts 1:8)*. It is appropriate to disobey government officials if they ask you to disobey God, which would require you to break one of God's commandments, not merely limit your preferences. Submit and defy accordingly.

4:23-24 When God moves, respond with praise and worship alongside other believers.

4:25-26 Cross-reference Psalm 2:1-2.

4:27-28 Choose to see life through the lens of God's plan vs. merely the actions of people.

4:29 They did not ask for the Sanhedrin to back off. They asked for boldness to continue sharing the gospel. We should challenge ourselves during hardship in the same way: pray for continued boldness more than you pray for the trial to end.

4:30 In addition to continued boldness to share, they prayed God would move in an immediate way to authenticate the truth of the gospel.

4:31 The Holy Spirit's filling was the result of their prayer. Pray for the Holy Spirit to fill you.

4:32-35 Here, we are given seven marks of a gospel church: **1) Unity** (*"one heart and soul"* - vs. 32); **2) Humility** (*"no one said that any of the things that belonged to him was his own"* - vs. 32); 3) **Equality** (*"but they had everything in common"* -vs. 32); **4) Great power to some** (*"with great power, the apostles..."* - vs. 33; **5) Gospel declared** (*"giving their testimony to the resurrection of the Lord Jesus"* - vs. 33; **6) Great grace to all** (*"great grace was upon them all"* - vs. 33); **7) Generosity** (*"there was not a needy person among them...it was distributed to each as any had need"* - vs. 34-35).

4:36-37 Barnabas will play an important role in the missionary journeys after Paul's conversion. It's important to note that the generosity we see on display from Barnabas and others was voluntary, not a requirement. Required generosity is not really generosity.

Acts 4

QUESTIONS

Icebreaker: There's something fun about seeing a "before and after" picture side by side of a total transformation *(maybe a house remodeling project or restoring an older car, etc.)* What's one of the most incredible "before and after" you've ever seen?

1. Why were the Sadducees "greatly annoyed" by Peter and John's preaching? (Acts 4:2) *(You can get a refresher on what the Sadducees believe in Matthew 22:23; Mark 12:18; Luke 20:27).*

2. Why is believing in Christ's death and resurrection so vital for a believer? Peter and John were put in prison over the sermon they preached, but people were also saved and many praised God. Kingdom results may sometimes come at a personal cost. What are some ways we can work to stay focused on God's mission instead of our own success?

3. Throughout the book of Acts, Luke rightly attributes the boldness we see to the work of the Holy Spirit. When it comes to the Holy Spirit's work in our lives, we often stifle it by ignoring Him or take credit for His work as if we did something in our own power instead of His. Which extreme do you lean to most often *(both in His work in your own life and observing the work of others)*? What's one thing you could do to acknowledge the work of the Holy Spirit around you more?

4. Read Acts 4:12 aloud. How does this one verse show that salvation is both inclusive and exclusive? *(Inclusive - available to all; exclusive - only available through Jesus.)* Have some empathy for a moment for some of your unbelieving friends. Why do you think some struggle with salvation being available to us exclusively through Jesus? How does the fact that salvation is available to all help with the difficulty some have in believing Jesus is the only way to heaven?

5. People can argue about theology and opinions, but it's hard to argue against a changed life. What's one way we can aim to live *changed?* What do you think is the most noticeable difference between your life before you accepted Christ and after you began following Him in obedience?

6. Re-read Acts 4:32-35. This passage gives us some marks of a gospel church. What are they? Which ones do you think are the hardest for a church to achieve, and why? Which mark do you need to work on the most personally?

Acts 5

COMMENTARY

5:1-8 We can learn a lot about Ananias' and Sapphira's character here that can serve as warning signs for us when our hearts are headed in a dangerous direction. 1) **Greed** *(lying about how much money they had)* 2) **Dishonesty** *(they conspired together to lie to their church leaders and church family)* 3) **Hypocrisy** *(they tried to get away with the appearance of generosity)* 4) **Fear of man** *(their partial donation and subsequent deception revealed that their reputation mattered more to them than being right before God).*

5:1-2 The donations the believers made were voluntary, not required. The issue is not about the size of their donation, but about their greed and dishonesty.

5:3-4 The willingness to deceive threatened the unity the believers were experiencing, but Peter chose to focus on Ananias' actions against God, not how Peter or anyone else had been wronged. When we become aware and are even affected by the sins of others, let's remember that although we may be caught in the crossfire, their offense is really against a holy God much more than an offense against us.

5:3 Note the phrase *"lie to the Holy Spirit."* There's a chance that Ananias and Sapphira could have gotten away with their deceit without the disciples finding out. But this wording reminds us that even when we are able to deceive people, we will never be able to deceive the Holy Spirit.

5:5 + 5:10 These verses often make people uncomfortable. But it's important that we wrestle with the tension that God's same power to perform miracles is the same power that will bring judgment. God is a God of mercy and grace, but verses like this remind us we cannot overlook His holiness. But this is an important distinction in that tension: God's judgment for sin isn't about His anger but rather about His holiness. Also, God's judgment for sin is real, but He also gave us Jesus so that we would have a way to stand rightly before Him. He knew we would never be holy enough to get to God on our own merit, so through Jesus, He made a way for us. So yes, God's judgment is real. But don't get so caught up on the uncomfortable aspect of judgment's realness that you forget the incredible comfort that Jesus is real too! So very real.

5:8 Sapphira was not held accountable for her husband's sin. Peter gave Sapphira an opportunity to tell the truth, and she repeated the lie.

5:13 Aim for the unbelievers in your life to respect you. God is the one who saves and softens hearts to hear and respond. But our goal should be to live in such a way that even if people disagree with how we believe, they respect the way we live. Respect is much more likely to leave the door open for their belief later.

5:14-16 The church in Jerusalem continued to grow, and their primary evangelistic strategy was meeting the real needs of the people. We live in a broken and hurting world, which means there is no shortage of needs around you. If you want to increase the number of people you get to show and share about Jesus, start by meeting their needs.

5:17 The Jewish leaders were jealous because of the *"success"* of the apostles' ministry, and they acted on their jealousy. Jealousy that is left unchecked typically will result in going further into sin, like the Jewish leaders having the apostles falsely arrested. Stop jealousy as quickly as you can. Especially if you find yourself becoming jealous of the work someone is doing in the Lord's name, repent of your jealousy, pray God will continue to bless their endeavors and get back to serving where God has placed you.

5:18 Putting the apostles in a public prison without any wrongdoing would have been a shame and scare tactic coinciding with a power move. Unfortunately, this is not an ancient problem. It still happens today. You can discern a lot about someone's motives from merely how conflict is handled. Matthew 18:15-20 reminds us that first, we should go directly to the believer who has offended us privately with the goal of restoration. Here, the quickness to take the conflict public exposes that the goal of the high priest and Sadducees was humiliation for the disciples and personal gain for themselves.

5:19-20 The apostles' circumstances would have been pretty bleak here. But even in the worst of circumstances, we must remind ourselves that there is no situation too hard for God to handle.

5:21 God provided a way for the apostles to be freed from prison, but they were still required to be bold enough to obey His command to go preach the gospel in the temple. We often pray for God to "open a door," but let's remember to also pray for courage to walk through the doors He opens. Let's aim for the kind of quick obedience displayed when the apostles immediately responded *"when they heard this."*

5:21-32 The human flesh longs for an explanation. And when God moves, the only explanation we should need is God Himself. So when others are longing for a human explanation, like the officers and high priest did, instead do what Peter and John did: point to God and share the gospel.

5:29 Few would admit to struggling with *"obeying men"* before God. But who we obey is best revealed by whose approval we seek and whose opinion most influences our actions. Obeying God will often require you to go against the current of culture – not in defiant opposition to the world, but in humble submission to God. Remember: Satan is our enemy. Culture may be headed in a different direction, but it's not our enemy. Culture provides our opportunity to share Christ. Make sure you are correctly identifying your real enemy.

5:33 What started as jealousy for the religious leaders has now escalated to the desire to commit murder. This is another example of how jealousy unchecked can often escalate into other sins.

5:34 Gamaliel was one of the teachers of Saul of Tarsus *(later to be known as the apostle Paul)* when he was studying to become a Pharisee.

5:35-39 Gamaliel points out two other examples of leaders who rose to great influence in the past, but after their death, their followers were quickly dismantled. He wisely discerns that religious movements that depend on human momentum will inevitably fail. On the contrary, what is of God will never fail, so attempts to oppose these movements will not work. Plus, he cautions them against being on the wrong side and ending up opposing God. Let this be your confidence: God cannot be overthrown, so the gospel cannot be stopped by mere men.

5:40 The apostles' obedience ultimately led to a severe beating. Remember that obedience does not equal earthly blessing, but eternal reward.

5:41 Their suffering prompted them to rejoice because they were worthy to suffer for the same cause Jesus did. Today, we often talk about suffering in conjunction with endurance, but here, suffering is linked to worship and joy.

5:42 I love the detail in acknowledging what was happening *"in the temple and from house to house."* Publicly and privately, the message and the goal was the same: to teach and preach who Jesus is.

What is the difference between preaching and teaching? Preaching is proclaiming the gospel. Teaching is explaining the gospel and how we live it out.

Acts 5

QUESTIONS

Icebreaker: In Acts 5, we meet a Pharisee named Gamileal, who was able to de-escalate a conflict with his wisdom. Who is the "Gamileal" in your life who always seems to know the right thing to say at the right time? Give us an example of a time they wowed you with their wise words.

1. What did Ananias and Sapphira do with the proceeds from selling a piece of their property? What do their actions reveal about their character that can be warning signs for us when our hearts are headed in the wrong direction? What do you think the phrase "lie to the Holy Spirit" in vs. 3 means? What can we learn from Peter choosing to point out how their sins offended God?

2. Do you have a similar reaction to the fate of Ananias and Sapphira as those who experienced this in real time? We're much more comfortable discussing God's grace and mercy than we are considering His holiness. But what happens if we choose to overlook God's holiness? How does the gospel bring more comfort than any discomfort over God's judgment for sin?

3. Read Acts 5:17-18 and Acts 5:33 aloud. The Saducees and the high priest first are jealous, and their jealousy ends up escalating to the desire to commit murder. What does this teach us about what happens when we allow ourselves to act on our jealousy? What are ways that we can work to dismantle our jealousy instead of allowing it to escalate?

4. What happened after the apostles were put in prison? What did God tell them to do, and how did they respond? *(Acts 5:19-20)* We often pray for God to "open a door," but we still need to have the courage to walk through the doors He opens. Is following through on obedience hard for you, even when it's clear God has made a way? Why or why not?

5. What were Peter and the apostles' response in vs. 29? What do you think it looks like to obey God instead of man? How do we make sure our response looks more like humble submission to God instead of merely defiant opposition to the world? Why does this matter?

6. Read Acts 5:35-39 aloud. What confidence does Gamaliel's advice give you in God and the gospel?

7. Read Acts 5:41 aloud. Do you typically think of suffering in terms of endurance or rejoicing? How do you think we get to a place where our suffering prompts us to rejoice?

Closing Prayer: Read Acts 5:42 and point out how the mission was the same both publicly *("in the temple")* and privately *("from house to house.")* Have the group members pick a partner (if your group is large) or share with the entire group one way they need prayer, support, and accountability for their public and private life to mirror each other more closely.

Acts 6-7

COMMENTARY

6:1 Because the Hellenists are Greek-speaking Gentiles/non-Jews, it's possible the oversight of caring for the widows could have been due to the language barrier, not purposeful neglect.

6:1-5 Growth is good, but growth alone will not solve all of your problems. In fact, be prepared for growth to *create* new problems for you to solve. But as the disciples do here, aim to address the new problems without losing your purpose. Also, recognize that *"increasing in number"* (vs. 1) will require more leaders. Therefore, you cannot sustain growth and the subsequent increased responsibility and workload alone.

6:3 This verse lists three main characteristics of those who should be chosen for greater leadership: good reputation, full of the Holy Spirit, and full of wisdom. Nothing personality-driven or skill-related is mentioned. As you serve the Lord, make these the character traits you desire and prioritize for yourself and new leaders you recruit.

6:4 The apostles delegated caring for the widows to more leaders because they were devoted to something else – *"to prayer and the ministry of the word."* When you delegate in Kingdom work, do so because you are devoted to another aspect of Kingdom work, not simply because you don't want to do it. Also, let's note that they were devoted to both prayer *and* preaching – not one or the other. Their private walk with the Lord and their public ministry were both made to be a priority.

6:6 When someone steps into a new assignment, get them started with prayer. Pray *for* them and as we see here, pray *with* them.

6:7	Look at the result of being willing to address the problem and expand the leadership: the Word of God continued to increase, the number of disciples multiplied greatly in Jerusalem, and many of the priests became obedient to the faith. Unresolved and unaddressed problems have a negative impact, but solved problems make greater things possible. Don't allow your pride or conflict avoidance to keep you from addressing problems that need to be solved.
6:5 + 6:8	The two phrases used to describe Stephen are *"full of faith and the Holy Spirit"* as well as *"full of grace and power."* If someone had to describe what you're full of, what words would they choose?
6:9-14	The accusations against Stephen confirm Jesus' words that His followers would be persecuted. *(See John 15:18-21.)*
6:11	The charges against Stephen were the same charges they made against Jesus. *(See Mark 14:63-64.)*
6:11 + 6:13	These verses describe how these men *"secretly instigated"* and *"set up false witnesses"* against Stephen. None of what they charged him with was true.
6:15	God was with Stephen. His face being *"like the face of an angel"* was a visible manifestation of the glory and presence of God. *(See Exodus 34:29-35 for when this happened to Moses and Matthew 17:2 for when this happened to Jesus.)*
7:2-53	This is the longest speech/sermon recorded in Acts. Stephen goes all the way back to Abraham and makes his way through Isaac, Jacob, Joseph, Moses, Joshua, David, Solomon, and finally to Jesus- to show how Jesus was the promised fulfillment from the beginning, not a deviation from God as he and the other disciples are being accused. The Bible is composed of many stories, but it's really one great story. It's a story about a loving God who goes to great lengths to save His people through His Son, Jesus. As you read throughout the Old Testament, look for how every story points to Jesus.

7:6 The 400 years refer to the time the Israelites spent as slaves in Egypt.

7:9-16 Stephen first begins to hint toward Jesus as he tells of how a whole family ended up being blessed by the brother [Joseph] they rejected. In the same way, we are all blessed through the One we rejected: Jesus.

7:22 Stephen describes Moses as being one who *"was mighty in his words and deeds"* while in reality, Moses had a stutter and had to speak to Pharaoh through Aaron *(Exodus 4:10-16)*. When you submit your weakness to God for Him to use, your legacy will be wrapped up more in what God did through your life than merely what you actually did.

7:35-36 The hints toward Jesus continue as Stephen points to Moses as a leader who Israel rejected once again, but this time, he goes further to make a connection between Moses as a *"ruler"* and a *"redeemer"* since he was the one to lead the Israelites out of slavery in Egypt.

7:37 Stephen is no longer hinting toward Jesus, but shows how Moses himself (the one Stephen is accused of speaking blasphemously against) prophesied about Jesus. *(See Deuteronomy 18:15 for the Old Testament passage Stephen references.)*

7:41 Israel has a history of idolatry. While we can mock Israel's worship of a golden calf, the same warning holds true for us: recognize your flesh's desire to be impressed by what you do over what God has done.

7:48 Some have used this verse to claim that attending church is not a necessary part of a believer's life. However, this verse is not condemning the church, but simply recognizing God cannot be contained to one building since He has always been at work among His people.

7:49-50 Cross-reference to Isaiah 66:1-2.

7:51 Stephen describes his persecutors as being *"uncircumcised in heart and ears,"* a strong comparison at the time but one that we would rarely hear today. Take some time to consider what it means to have a "circumcised" heart and ears. Our goal should be to have a heart that remains soft for God and others and to listen, trust, and obey God.

7:51-53 Stephen closes his argument with the fact that Judaism began long before Moses or the temple and that they killed the One [Jesus] that all the prophets pointed to. Hence, they are the ones who have abandoned God and His promises, not Stephen and the disciples of Jesus. Stephen's historical account illustrates Israel's constant rejection of God's chosen leaders. He is using this last opportunity to share his convictions and pleads with his persecutors to abandon their patterns of rejection.

7:52 By referring to Jesus as the "Righteous One," Stephen clearly identifies Jesus as God's Son.

7:53 Stephen had to have known his death would likely follow these words. Where did he get this kind of confidence? 1) God's very presence. 2) The power of the Holy Spirit. 3) A strong faith foundation built over time to be able to see how God has continued to be faithful to keep His promises through His work from the beginning. The same things are what will give us confidence as we live for the Lord today.

7:53-54 Human flesh gravitates toward self-preservation, but the spirit longs for God. Here, moments before being dragged and stoned, Stephen saw God's glory coming more than he saw his own death coming.

7:55-56 There are about 16 New Testament references to Jesus or the Son of Man being at God's right hand. Four references describe Jesus as being "at" God's right hand *(Acts 2:33, Acts 5:31; Romans 8:34; 1 Peter 3:22)*. The remaining references describe Him as seated *(Matthew 26:64; Mark 14:62, Mark 16:19; Luke 22:69; Acts 2:34; Ephesians 1:20; Colossians 3:1; Hebrews 1:3, Hebrews 8:1, Hebrews 10:12, and Hebrews 12:2)*. Acts 7:55-56 is unique because it's the sole reference that describes the Son of Man as *"standing"* at the right hand of God, not just once but twice. The ideas as to why Stephen saw Jesus standing include: 1) He once stood trial before the Sanhedrin guilty, and now, He stands victorious. 2) Jesus stands with those who testify about Him. 3) Jesus is welcoming Stephen into heaven.

7:58 This is the first mention of Saul of Tarsus. The fact that he didn't participate in the stoning, but the garments were laid at his feet showed that he was an up and coming leader among the Pharisees. Let this sink in: the man God would later use to reach the Gentiles with the gospel, who wrote the majority of the New Testament, and who is remembered for being the greatest missionary of all time, participated in murdering Stephen, the first martyr after Jesus' resurrection. This is a powerful example of how no one can out sin God's love and grace.

7:59-60 Stephen has two prayers on his lips as he dies: *"Receive my spirit"* and *"Do not hold this sin against them"* - the same prayers Jesus had on the cross. See Luke 23:34 and Luke 23:46.

7:60 *"Fell asleep"* is a common term that Christians used for death at this time, implying that this life is not the end since we have the assurance of eternal life through Christ.

Acts 6-7

QUESTIONS

Icebreaker: In the beginning of Acts 6, as the disciples were growing and there were more needs to be met, we see the apostles discussing how to delegate certain tasks to other leaders so they could continue to care for the church well. When your responsibilities increase, who is someone in your life you can always count on to jump in and share the load?

1. The disciples were tasked with picking seven men who would be chosen for greater leadership to meet the physical needs of the people. What were the three characteristics Acts 6:3 lists these men need to have? Do you think those characteristics are still ones that would work to determine who's ready to serve the Lord today?

2. When the church grows, it creates more needs to be met, which cannot be met by the pastors alone. More people coming to your church means more people are needed to serve at your church. What ministry area do you currently serve in, or what need have you noticed/been made aware of recently at your church where you can jump in and help share the load?

3. Read Acts 6:7 aloud. What three results came from the disciples' willingness to address the problem they were made aware of? Do you tend to view solving problems as positive or negative? For example, when someone comes to you and shares something you're responsible for that isn't being done, is your first reaction to try to solve the problem, or do you get defensive of your work/time or desire to avoid conflict?

4. Read Acts 6:5 and Acts 6:8 aloud. Both verses contain descriptions of Stephen. What four things do these two verses list that Stephen was full of? If others were to describe what you're full of, what words do you think they would choose? What words would you desire to be chosen?

5. The Bible is composed of many stories, but it's really one great story. It's a story about a loving God who goes to great lengths to save His people through His Son, Jesus. What parallels to Jesus do you see through the Old Testament stories Stephen shares and through Stephen's trial and death?

6. God made our bodies incredibly instinctive to protect themselves from harm. Under normal circumstances, the moments before being stoned would be full of terror and fighting to stay alive. Read Acts 7:54-56 aloud. Despite what was happening around Stephen, what was he focused on? Also, the New Testament often uses the phrase "fell asleep" to record death. What does that phrase remind us as believers who have eternal life in Christ?

7. Have you ever heard someone say that they need to "clean themselves up" before they can come to church? Or have you ever felt like your sins are so great that there's just no way God could love you or forgive you? How does the fact that God used Saul, one of the worst persecutors of Christians, to later write the majority of the New Testament and dedicate his life to sharing the gospel- speak truth over these fears and insecurities you may have?

Acts 8-9

COMMENTARY

8:1 It's hard to look at the *"great persecution"* against the church that began with the martyrdom of Stephen as a blessing, but note the result of the persecution marked here: *"they were all scattered throughout the regions of Judea and Samaria."* The persecution led to the fulfillment of Acts 1:8, where believers were moved to the specific places they were called to take the gospel. Discomfort and setbacks do not mean God is not moving. Trust Him and His plan.

8:3 Prior to Stephen's death, followers of Jesus were thrown in prison largely due to jealousy and power dynamics. After Stephen's death, however, the persecution spread to all who merely believed in Jesus, not just when Jews felt threatened by Christians receiving too much attention.

8:4 Those who were scattered to new areas did not hide, pout, or fear - they preached the Word. Most of us have never been faced with the potential of this magnitude for persecution, yet we have cowered over far less push back. Desire the boldness on display by the believers here to proclaim the word of the Lord

8:6 The crowds paid attention to Philip *"when they heard him **and** saw the signs that he did."* People are most likely to pay attention to the gospel and believe when your words and actions align.

8:6-8 Hearing the Word of God and seeing the works of God produced joy throughout the city. Want to see more joy in your city? Make it a priority to help your city hear the Word of God and see the work of God.

8:9-12 Simon amazed the crowds with his magic, but Philip was just as captivating with the message of the gospel. Most people you meet have had "run-ins" with religion, but every other major world religion is rooted in what you have to do to get to heaven. Christianity is rooted in what Jesus has already done. Never underestimate the power of sharing the simple message of God's overwhelming grace.

8:13 Simon's steps give us a great road-map to follow for those we evangelize and disciple: 1) Salvation through belief. 2) Baptism as their first step of obedience and an outward expression of the change that has occurred on the inside. 3) Continue discipling them.

8:14-17 The Samaritans and Jews had been long-time enemies. Sending Peter and John to Samaria when the apostles heard the Samaritans had accepted Christ shows how the power of the gospel compelled them to unite despite prejudices of the past. When there are groups of believers you struggle to pursue unity with, let the gospel be bigger than any other issue. When believers lose their unity, 100% of the time, something has become more important than Jesus.

8:18-19 God's gifts - from salvation to spiritual gifts - cannot be bought. God's gifts are truly gifts in every sense - freely given. The challenge is to accept God's free gift without drifting into spiritual laziness. Dallas Williard once explained the difference this way: *"Grace is not opposed to effort. Grace is opposed to earning."*

8:20-23 Peter's rebuke of Simon is strong here, but is spot on. The sins that often go unaddressed are the ones that are wrapped up in motive more than action. Simon wanted to do something for God, which is good, but his motives revealed his heart wasn't right before the Lord. Remember to examine your motives, not just your words or actions. And just as Peter encouraged Simon, repent quickly and ask God for forgiveness.

8:24 It would be easy to criticize Simon for his actions here, but let's remember a few things: 1) Simon is a newly converted Christian. Yes, believers are free from condemnation in Christ *(Romans 8:1)*, but that doesn't mean that we won't ever stumble into sin. Remember to exercise a lot of patience for the younger believers in your life and don't write them off for their mistakes, just like God doesn't write you off for yours. 2) Simon responds to the rebuke in humility by asking for prayer. I love how Eugene Peterson describes following Christ as a *"long obedience in the same direction."* Simon may have momentarily veered off course, but the correction got him back on course in the right direction. When you realize you've veered from God's best, repent to God first, and ask other believers to pray for you.

8:26-27 It would not have made logical sense for Philip to go to the desert. But as we're going to see, he willingly obeys and God shows up! Don't wait to obey when God's call and human logic align. Obey God fully, obey Him right away, and expect Him to show up with Kingdom results.

8:28-39 There is so much unknown here about how this situation occurred. First of all, why was an Ethiopian concerned enough to read Hebrew Scriptures? How did he get a copy of them in the first place? Philip got to be there for the eunuch's conversion and baptism, but likely, there were other believers who invested in this man's life before he met Philip. Reminder for us: you may not get to see the impact of your faith or the fruit that occurs from the gospel seeds that you plant in the lives of others, but that doesn't mean God won't use them in His time and in His way. And even though we don't know the names of those who invested in the Ethiopian eunuch prior to him meeting Philip in the desert, we can trust those believers, and their actions are very known to the Lord.

8:29 The Spirit still speaks, and the Spirit still prompts. Remember that if you are in Christ, the Holy Spirit *(the full Holy Spirit - there's no such thing as half Holy Spirit or Holy Spirit Jr.!)* lives in you. Are you listening for Him, and when He speaks, will you obey?

8:31 As an Ethiopian eunuch, this man was a high-ranking government official. But despite his title, power, and influence, he shows great humility in admitting he doesn't understand what he's reading. Humility is required for salvation and continued belief.

8:32-33 Cross-reference to Isaiah 53:7-8.

8:32-35 The prophet Isaiah ministered faithfully for years and saw very few repent and choose God during his life. But here, about 800 years later, his words are used to help the Ethiopian eunuch accept Christ as the Lord of his life. We live in a world that praises productivity and results that we can measure, but when it comes to the ways we live for the Lord, we need to have a "longer than a lifetime" view for how our lives can and will be used by God. Stay faithful to God and what He calls you to do, and trust that as Isaiah said himself, God's Word never returns void *(Isaiah 55:11)*.

8:35 When you share the gospel with someone, keep it simple. Start with Scripture and make Jesus the focus.

8:36-39 This sentence doesn't seem extraordinary unless we remember that they are in the desert! How likely do you think it would be to stumble upon a large enough body of water that would have been big enough for Philip to *"come up out of the water?"* Probably slim to none - but God provided! As you are doing ministry, remind yourself that conditions don't matter. God will provide what is necessary for ministry.

8:37 The eunuch's excitement is contagious. He can't wait to obey! Transparently, obedience is something that we can begin to view begrudgingly. One of the easiest ways to keep yourself excited about following God is by surrounding yourself with new believers and being a part of others' salvation stories. If you ever start to view obeying God as more of a burden than a blessing, ask yourself when the last time was that you were around someone who just started following the Lord or you got to be there when someone accepted Christ as their Savior. Keep your own grace fresh by seeing His fresh grace for others.

8:39-40 Luke reports this pretty matter-of-fact, but this is another miracle without much explanation. Philip straight up disappears after the Ethiopian eunuch is baptized, and neither Philip nor the eunuch seem to be surprised or bothered by this at all! 1) For the eunuch, he has Jesus, which is what he needs to rejoice and move forward in his faith. Philip didn't make it about Philip, so the eunuch didn't either. 2) Philip finds himself in a completely new city, and instead of wondering how he got there or why God chose to move him when He did so abruptly, he just continued to preach as he passed through new towns. I wonder how much

Kingdom energy gets wasted because we long to know why or we believe God owes us some form of explanation. What if we just moved on and continued the mission - trusting God has the whys and answers, so we don't have to?

9:1-18 This incredible redemption story of Saul reveals so much to us about God's grace and illustrates the truth Saul would later write in Romans 5:8: *"But God demonstrates his own love for us in this: While we were still sinners, Christ died for us."* Regardless of how you have responded to God or the way you currently may be living right now, He loves you, He sees you as His child, and He desires a relationship with you. He may not blind you on the Damascus road to get to you, but He is always pursuing you.

9:2 Before the term "Christian" is used, followers of Jesus were referred to as belonging to "the Way." In John 14:6, Jesus says, *"I am the way, and the truth, and the life. No one comes to the Father except through Me."*

9:4 Notice that Jesus doesn't say, "Why are you persecuting *them*?" But rather, He asks Saul, *"Why are you persecuting Me?"* This one word provides a powerful glimpse into how closely Jesus identifies Himself with us when we believe in Him and follow Him.

9:7 There were witnesses to Saul's encounter with Jesus on the road to Damascus. The men traveling with Saul could not see anyone, but they heard the voice speaking to him. This is just another example of how our faith is backed up with facts and based on real events that really happened.

9:9 Sometimes, people take stories like this one and claim instances like Paul's blindness as evidence that God was punishing him for his actions. *(Other examples are Jonah's three days in the belly of a fish or Zechariah's inability to speak in Luke 1.)* But because God's plan is to be with us, punishment is never His end goal, but restoration. Paul's temporary blindness was more to allow Paul time to reflect than simply a punishment.

9:10 These four words make a beautiful prayer anytime and anywhere: *"Here I am, Lord."*

9:10-17 Ananias knew Saul had been persecuting Christians, and he knew that in the city where they were, Saul had the authority to throw him in prison simply for being a follower of Jesus. Ananias had real reasons to fear Saul, so he was honest with God about his fears. God revealed His plan for Saul, and Ananias chose to follow God instead of following his fear. When you fear what God is calling you to do, be honest with God, listen for His truth, and choose to follow God instead of your fear.

9:17 Ananias greets Saul as "Brother Saul." Keep in mind that all that's happened at this point is Saul's salvation. He has not preached, renounced his former actions, or done anything yet to demonstrate his faith in Christ. Salvation is the mark that makes us spiritual siblings. Nothing more and nothing less.

9:18 Sometimes, we have to wait on the Lord. Sometimes, He acts immediately. The different pace He chooses between circumstances actually protects our dependence on Him and increases our faith in Him as we trust Him for every step instead of simply trusting in outcomes and methods.

9:20 Saul went from persecuting Christians to proclaiming Jesus immediately after his salvation. You don't have to wait to be Christ's witness. As soon as you put your faith in Jesus, you can begin telling others about Him.

9:21 People were amazed by the change in Saul. Maybe the changes in you aren't as drastic, but without question, there are still changes. Stay in awe of what Christ has done for you by reminding yourself and those around you of the difference following Jesus makes in your life.

9:22 Saul continued to increase in strength as he began doing the work of God. When you desire your faith to increase, put your faith into practice and join God at work. Wherever you are, God is already at work, so you don't have to put pressure on yourself to begin the work. You get to join God where He's already working.

9:23 Remember Gamileal's speech that a true movement of God cannot be stopped? *(Acts 5:33-39)*. Because the gospel cannot

	be stopped, be prepared for its enemies to resort to extreme measures, like the Jews' plan to kill Saul.
9:24-25 + 9:29-30	Because many oppose the gospel, we can expect conflict to occur. These two instances serve as our reminder that we are not required to fight every battle. If the Holy Spirit reveals danger to you and does not ask you to stay, follow His prompting and don't engage the fight.
9:26	We've seen a lot of growth in the disciples' boldness throughout the book of Acts, but spiritual growth doesn't equal spiritual perfection. Similar to Ananias' objections, they knew what they had seen of Saul, so his conversion was hard to believe. When you find yourself doubting what the Holy Spirit has done in someone else's life, just remember the change that He has made in yours.
9:27-28	Barnabas is first mentioned in Acts 4:36 when he sells a property and brings the money to the apostles. That verse also tells us that his real name is Joseph. Barnabas, which means *"son of encouragement"* is a nickname. Nicknames are earned, and here, we see why. Barnabas believed Saul when none of the other apostles did. But also, the apostles change their minds about Saul when Barnabas is the one to affirm his testimony and ministry. Two takeaways for us: 1) Take risks to invest in those who claim Christ, even if there's no evidence to prove you should. 2) Aim to have the kind of character that encourages others to believe the best in someone else simply because you do.
9:31	Multiplication is different from addition. Addition implies a few people are doing the work to add to the following, but multiplication indicates everyone is working together to multiply God's mission. This verse breaks down the four things that are needed for multiplication to occur: 1) peace; 2) being built up; 3) walking in fear of the Lord; 4) walking in the comfort of the Holy Spirit.
9:32-35	As Peter does here, recognize Jesus for everything you're able to do for the Kingdom. It's His power at work within you, not just you. This is not only beneficial for keeping your own pride in check, but notice that the people of Lydda and Sharon were

9:36-39 Tabitha is introduced as a disciple who did many good things for others. Our actions will determine how we are remembered.

9:40-42 God's miracles are never just about the miracle, but His miracles point us back to God Himself. While there are many miracles throughout the book of Acts, only believers are raised from the dead. This is yet another reminder that in Christ, this life is not the end. And when people heard about Tabitha coming back to life, many were saved. Be in awe of God, not just the miracles He does.

9:43 As a tanner, Simon's job would have made him often come in contact with dead animals. Simon would have been "unclean" according to Old Testament law. Peter's willingness to stay with Simon shows he is losing his prejudice and embracing the new covenant we have with Christ instead of aiming to also live under the law.

Acts 8-9

QUESTIONS

Icebreaker: Both Ananias and Barnabas had real reasons to fear Saul, but they chose to follow God instead of giving into following their fear. Can you remember a time in your life when you were afraid, but your faith in God gave you the courage to press on anyway? When was it, and how did God show up for you?

1. Read Acts 8:1 and Acts 1:8 aloud. How did the great persecution Christians began to endure recorded in Acts 8 help fulfill the assignment given to them in Acts 1? What does this teach us about the circumstances we find ourselves in that human logic would define as a setback?

2. Read Acts 8:6-8 aloud. What two things contributed to bringing much joy to the city? No matter where you live, I'm sure your city could use more joy. How can you prioritize bringing the Word of God and the works of God into the place where you live?

3. How hard is it to fight against the human logic side of our brains that desires that all the right conditions be in place before we attempt to minister to others? We serve a God who made a body of water appear in the desert so Philip could baptize the Ethiopian eunuch! How can we increase our trust that God will provide the right conditions for ministry if we will just be willing to obey?

4. Read Acts 9:4 aloud. Who does Jesus say Saul was persecuting? Who was Saul actually persecuting? How does the way Jesus views Saul's persecution of Christians reveal the way He sees those who believe in and follow Him?

5. When God first instructs Ananias concerning Saul *(Acts 9:11-15)*, Ananias expresses to God his fear of Saul and his potential arrest if he goes to him. God tells Ananias of His plans for Saul to take the gospel to the Gentiles, so Ananias chooses to trust God and go meet Saul. What does this teach us about how honest we can be with God in prayer and about how our faith should speak into our fears?

6. In Acts 9:17, how does Ananias greet Saul? At this point, what had Saul done to show that his conversion was genuine? What does this teach us about salvation and how we should view others who believe in Jesus?

7. Go back and read Acts 4:36, when we are first introduced to Barnabas. Now consider how Barnabas is the one to bring Saul to the disciples when they were afraid to meet with him. How does this situation prove Barnabas earned his nickname genuinely? What can we learn from how Barnabas helped Saul?

Acts 10-11

COMMENTARY

10:1-2 Cornelius was described as a devout man, which meant he feared God and led his family to fear God as well. He gave generously to the poor, and he prayed continuously. But even with all of these good traits, Cornelius was still lost without Christ. This serves as a reminder for us that it's Christ who gives us the ability to stand rightly before God, not our devout traits. And this also reminds us that those who are lost aren't just those people who are evil, but also includes good people who simply don't have faith in Jesus.

10:3-6 What matters here is that we realize what the angel does *not* say to Cornelius as much as we pay attention to what the angel does say. The angel could have shared the gospel with Cornelius himself, but instead, the angel instructs Cornelius to find Peter so Peter could be the one to tell Cornelius the good news about Jesus. Matthew 28:19-20 and Acts 1:8 both reiterate that sharing the gospel with others is a responsibility given by God to those who already believe. And even though God could have chosen to spread the gospel another way, He chose us, and this exchange between the angel and Cornelius points back to that foundational truth.

10:3-8 Even though Cornelius did not know Christ, He sought after God. The angel sent Cornelius to Peter for the purpose of Cornelius hearing and believing the gospel. Review the note on Acts 4:12 concerning the exclusivity of salvation through faith in Jesus alone. While human logic may see that as limiting, the story of Cornelius illustrates that while Jesus is the only way to get to God, God will go to great lengths to reveal Jesus to those who seek Him.

10:9-16 Up until Jesus comes on the scene, God's chosen people have been clearly identified as Israel/Jews. There were hundreds of laws concerning what animals were deemed clean and unclean. *(For a glimpse, cross-reference to Leviticus 11:2-47.)* The voice that instructed Peter in the midst of the vision to kill and eat the unclean animals *(animals that he's instructed not to call common since God has made them clean)* is evidence that God is revealing to Peter His plans to reach the Gentiles *(non-Jews)* with the gospel.

10:17-21 God uses visions to communicate to both Cornelius and Peter. There is divine intervention from God to speak to both of them, but both men still have to act on what God revealed to them in each vision. Our confidence to act on what God says can come from a place of believing that when God goes before us, He will also go before others, just as He prepared Cornelius for Peter and Peter for Cornelius.

10:22 Cornelius appeared to have it all. He was a successful, upright, and God-fearing man who was well-spoken of by the whole Jewish nation, but he lacked the gospel. As much good as Cornelius did, he did not have Christ. The good people around you who do not have Jesus are not saved. Sometimes, those conversations seem more uncomfortable to have than sharing the gospel with someone who appears to be far from the Lord. But if someone doesn't know the gospel, despite how put together their life may appear, they need the good news of Jesus.

10:25-26 When you speak and act under the influence of the Holy Spirit, some may put unnecessary emphasis on you. Whether they believe you're a powerful speaker or they're amazed by your actions, human logic will focus on what is seen *(you)* rather than what is unseen *(God)*. As Peter does here, put an end to any attention you're given, not in a shaming way, but in a way that ensures praise is reserved for God alone.

10:28 This verse shows us how Peter interprets and understands the vision God gave him.

10:29 Peter had been raised in the faith to believe that certain animals were clean or unclean, and that the Jews were God's chosen people. Here, we see that God has transformed Peter's mind, heart, and subsequent actions through the gospel. Transparently, human logic and tradition can impact our beliefs more than we'd like to acknowledge. So a question worth asking ourselves is, "Are you open to God changing your mind?" My pastor, Bruce Frank, often puts it this way: "When God and I disagree, He's right, I'm wrong, and by the grace of God, I can change."

10:31 Just as the angel told Cornelius, remember that God hears your prayers and He remembers what you do for Him, even if it's an act that no one else sees.

10:33 Whenever we hear someone preach, let's remember what it is. This is not merely someone exercising their spiritual gift or us checking off one of the boxes on our spiritual checklist. Preaching occurs when people gather in God's presence to hear what the Lord has commanded to be said. Let's not allow ourselves to dilute preaching to anything else.

10:34-43 Peter began with the truth God communicated to him in the vision– God shows no partiality - the gospel is for everyone. Then he goes back and lays the foundation for the gospel. We must remember that everything "new" God shows us that comes from Him will emphasize the truth of the gospel and fit into the framework of the gospel.

10:38 *"For God was with Him."* It was true then, and it should be our aim today as well.

10:41 Peter's emphasis that Jesus ate and drank with his disciples proved it was not merely Jesus' Spirit who appeared to the disciples, but truly Jesus, in human form, raised from the dead.

10:44 We are incapable of manufacturing the Holy Spirit's words and works on our own. Pay attention when the Spirit moves.

10:44-48 Just a few days ago, Peter believed the Gentiles were unclean. Now, he's preaching to them, seeing the Spirit move in their hearts, and calling for them to be baptized in the name of Jesus Christ. When you do the work of God, the most powerful work that will be done won't just be in what you do - but the work God does in you as you work with Him. Don't just look for God's work to appear in external results, but pay attention to how He's working in you and in those around you too.

10:1-48 Cornelius needed the gospel, and Peter needed to understand the gospel is also for the Gentiles. God used the men in one another's lives to meet both of their needs at the same time. God starts working in you at salvation, but He never stops working in you either. This side of heaven, we never reach a place where God is not growing us to be more like Christ. Be sensitive to how God is growing you, and change accordingly.

11:1 Before Peter is able to make it back to Jerusalem, word has gotten back to the believers there about the Gentiles receiving the word of God. Just as Peter had to learn and grow to realize the gospel is for the Gentiles too, Peter will now need to lead the Jews through this understanding as well.

11:2 You can miss the big blessing of seeing God at work if the first lens you operate through is that of a critical spirit. Be slow to criticize.

11:4 It's easy to get defensive when others disagree with our actions. But notice how Peter didn't begin his defense by defending his actions. He began with God's actions. When someone disagrees with you and brings it to your attention, make every effort to not merely defend your actions, but point to God's action that prompted your response.

11:12 "Making no distinction" didn't mean there weren't differences. It simply meant that there was to be no discrimination over differences that God didn't recognize. In its simplest form, we are all sinners in front of a holy God. And Jesus is the only way to reconcile our sin with God's holiness.

11:5-18 As we've already seen, even as we pursue unity, we are still likely to encounter times when we disagree with other believers, just as the believers in Jerusalem disagreed with Peter's actions initially. So when these times occur, this story gives us an example of how we should respond: 1) Hear someone out before you judge them. Listen for God's truth in what the other person shares. 2) Arguments don't have to be loud. If you hear God's truth in what they share, keep quiet. Otherwise, you'll end up arguing for the sake of trying to be right instead of acknowledging the other person is right. 3) You can glorify God for realizing you were wrong and being grateful He revealed what is right to you.

11:20 God has revealed separately that the gospel is for the Gentiles four times: 1) To Ananias concerning Paul (Acts 9:15), 2) to Peter in his vision in Acts 10, 3) to the Jerusalem church through Peter (Acts 11), and in this verse, through Cyprus and Cyrene at the Church of Antioch. *(Hellenists were Greeks, not Jews.)* Big movements of God will require many of his servants to be stirred and prompted to the same work. In a world where more and more "branding" and "brand protection" are seeping into ministry circles and conversations, we need to stop and recognize that God's servants should sound alike and do similar work.

11:21 Big growth happened in the church because of God's power alone. Just as Luke didn't give credit anywhere else, we must ensure we credit God alone when He moves among His people.

11:23 If you ever want to know if you bend toward religion or the gospel, just ask yourself if seeing God's grace makes you joyful. Religion gets angry over grace, and the gospel rejoices over grace. Religion wants grace to be deserved or earned, but that's the opposite of the gospel. Barnabas also doesn't stop at being glad about God's grace, but he encourages them to remain in faith. We get to come to Jesus as we are, but coming to Jesus also means we don't stay as we are. Christ changes you to be more like Him, and as Barnabas encourages the believers at Antioch, we must be purposeful in our pursuit of Him.

11:25-26 It's easy to feel like the entire book of Acts happens quickly, but this verse should force us to slow down our timelines. Saul and Barnabas spent an entire year teaching the new believers in Antioch. In your zeal and excitement to reach others with the good news of the gospel, remember to teach those you are able to reach. And recognize that teaching is done over time with repetition. It's not merely quick words once, but an investment you willingly make over and over again.

11:26 *"They were first called Christians"* implies this was likely a name that was given to them by others, not a name that they adopted for themselves. In fact, both the Bible *(cross-reference to 1 Peter 4:16)* and history suggests that this was probably created as a mocking insult.

11:27-30 Don't miss this. The new church in Antioch of all new believers is sending help to the established church in Judea. Discipleship is a two-way street. Even if you have been walking with Christ longer, that doesn't mean you can't be blessed, strengthened, and ministered to by a younger believer. *(Cross-reference to 1 Timothy 4:12).*

Acts 10-11

QUESTIONS

Icebreaker: In these chapters, we see the Jewish people adopting a major change by realizing the gospel is for everyone, not just for the people of Israel. Most often, how do you respond to change? Do you like change, or do you typically resist change at first?

1. Read Acts 10:2 aloud. What were the four traits used to emphasize that Cornelius was a devout man? But even with all of these good traits, what is Cornelius missing? What does this remind us about our own "good traits" and about those around us who are good people but don't know Jesus? Do you think it's easier or harder to share the gospel with those whose lives make it appear like they're already a good person? Why?

2. Why do you think the angel wanted Peter to share the gospel with Cornelius, and the angel didn't simply share the gospel with Cornelius instead? God could choose another way to spread the gospel to the ends of the earth, and yet, He chose us. Read Matthew 28:19-20 and Acts 1:8 to remind believers of the role we're called to play in sharing the gospel with others.

3. Transparently, human logic and tradition can impact our beliefs more than we'd like to acknowledge. How hard is it for God to change your mind? How do you handle the times when you and God disagree?

4. Cornelius needed the gospel, and Peter needed to understand the gospel is also for the Gentiles. God used the men in one another's lives to accomplish both at the same time. God starts working in you at salvation, but He never stops working in you either. How is God growing you right now? What is He working to teach you and show you?

5. Just as Peter had to learn and grow to realize the gospel is for the Gentiles too, Peter will now need to lead the Jews through this understanding as well. Acts 11:2 lets us see Peter has his work cut out for him, as he is immediately met with criticism. His critics have

missed the big blessing of seeing God at work in the Gentiles and the spreading of the gospel! Are you quick or slow to criticize? And in the moments when our initial response is wrong, what can we learn from the response of the church in Judea? *(See Acts 11:18)*.

6. Read Acts 11:25-26. Saul and Barnabas spent an entire year teaching the new believers in Antioch. In your zeal and excitement to reach others with the good news of the gospel, do you remember to take the time to teach those you reach? What does teaching those you reach look like where God has you now?

7. Read Acts 11:27-30. Even if you have been walking with Christ longer, that doesn't mean you can't be blessed, strengthened, and ministered to by a younger believer. Or just because you're newer in your faith, that doesn't mean God can't use you in the life of someone who has been following Christ longer than you. Can you share a story of a time God used you as a young believer, or a time when a younger believer ministered to you?

Acts 12-13

COMMENTARY

12:1-11 James was killed, and God chose to rescue Peter from prison. Seeing the outcome of these two apostles' lives recorded so closely together is a powerful reminder that our circumstances do not dictate God's love for us. God loved both James and Peter. In the tough moments that you do not understand, remind yourself that you can always trust God, and no matter what, you can be confident He loves you.

12:2 Jesus predicted James would suffer as He did. Cross-reference to Mark 10:32-45.

12:3 Herod had James killed and *"when he saw that it pleased the Jews,"* he arrested Peter too. Pleasing people is a dangerous motive. Also, pleasing people typically has roots in selfishness. History points to the idea that Herod [Herod Agrippa 1] was aiming for kingdom expansion so that the territory he ruled over would be the same as his grandfather's, Herod the Great. So he was not merely pleasing people to make them happy, but he was looking to please himself by increasing his power too. When pleasing people pops up in your life, dig deeper to find the root of selfishness.

12:3-4 The days of Unleavened Bread were the seven days following Passover. These days were considered holy, so that's why Herod had Peter arrested and put in prison, but not immediately executed. An execution during these days, according to rules and custom, would have defiled the holy celebration. The flaw in this is that God is the One who is holy, and His holiness doesn't change based on what day of the year it is. We may be drifting to a rules mindset over a relationship with God if we change the way we act or modify the words we use in certain places or on certain days only. Recognize God as holy, and let His holiness speak over every moment of your life.

12:4 Four squads of soldiers was a common Roman practice, so there would be four soldiers for each three-hour shift during the night. Because the soldiers guarding Peter would have been fresh for their shift, and Peter would have been outnumbered one to four, this further emphasizes God's solo role in the miracle of Peter's escape from prison.

12:5 All prayer is powerful simply because no matter where we are, we can actually talk to God, and He hears us. I love how this verse, though, emphasizes that earnest prayer was being made for Peter to God by the church. Earnest prayer implies their prayers were urgent and fervent. Go to God in prayer often, remembering that there's nothing He can't do. They had just seen James die, but they still believed that God could rescue Peter; so they prayed. Also, this wasn't a few prayers lifted up by church leaders; instead, the whole church prayed in unity to their God they were confident *could* rescue Peter. Don't miss the blessing of praying in unity with other believers to our great God who can do the impossible.

12:6 These details further display God's power. Peter was sleeping between two guards, bound by two chains, and there were additional guards at the door.

12:6-11 The angel was the one who was physically with Peter, but Peter recognized the angel as God's servant and God as the One who delivered him. Peter was grateful for the angel, but he praised God.

12:12-16 The people gathered were praying God would rescue Peter, yet they were still surprised when God actually rescued him! Pray confidently to God, and expect a response. It may not always be the answer you want, but you can always expect God to respond when you pray.

12:18-19 This was another common Roman practice: guards who lost their prisoners were subject to the same sentence as the prisoner. This confirms that Herod's plans were not merely to arrest Peter, but also to kill him.

12:20-22 The people's praise of Herod was mere flattery, not genuine admiration. Their country depended on Herod for food to eat, so

12:23 Pride is a serious sin, but it's one we often handle lightly. See the note on Acts 10:26 as a reminder of how Peter handled attention when others attempted to give him the glory that God deserved. Herod is not punished for the actions of other people praising him, but his punishment is because he didn't turn their praise into giving God glory. Stop your pride *(and the subsequent damage it does!)* with worship to God.

12:24 A lot has happened in this chapter. James has been killed, Peter has been rescued, and Herod has also died. And while there's a variety of circumstances that stir up many different emotions, the church still has momentum. Kingdom growth does not depend on circumstances, but on God alone.

13:1 I love that Luke takes the time to give us a peak of the diversity of the people of the church at Antioch. But because they had Jesus in common, they could worship, fast, and pray together. If we try to build common ground with other believers on something other than Jesus, unity will break down at some point.

13:2-3 Commission others to go and do God's work. Pray for them and find ways to show your support, as the church at Antioch did for Barnabas and Saul.

13:3 A note to those who serve in ministry: Before being sent for the work, the Holy Spirit acknowledged Barnabas and Saul were *"set apart for Me."* Have a "for God" approach to the work He has called you to instead of simply a "for the work" mindset.

13:4 At the end of every church gathering, one of our pastors will always say, *"You are loved and you are sent."* Wherever God has you, live sent by the Holy Spirit, just as Luke acknowledged in his retelling of Saul and Barnabas.

13:5 Since Jews already believed in the Old Testament, the synagogues were a good place to start each time they arrived in a new place.

13:8 Because we have a real enemy, we can always expect opposition in doing God's work.

13:9 This is the first time it's mentioned that Saul also goes by Paul, which is what we typically refer to him as now. It was common for Jews who were also Roman citizens *(which Paul was)* to have both a Jewish name and a Roman name. Saul was his Jewish name, and Paul was his Roman name. Since they are now ministering in Gentile territory, it's a common thought that this is why Paul chose to go by his Roman name instead of his Jewish name. We're never given an explanation; that's simply our best guess. But I do think there's something else here that I'll always wonder about too. Historically, Saul was the name of the first king of Israel, so Saul had a regal connotation. But Paul means small or humble. Again, we can't draw any conclusions for certain, but perhaps this man who used to spend his days persecuting Christians, who was once filled with pride and selfish ambition, would want the reminder every time his name was uttered of who he is in light of who Christ is. Powerful!

13:2,4,9 Luke always credits the Holy Spirit for the movements of man under God's direction.

13:9-12 Miracles in the book of Acts, like the magician's blindness, are never just about the miracle but about salvation. The proconsul wasn't astonished by Paul, but believed and was astonished *"at the teaching of the Lord."*

13:13 Luke acknowledges quickly that John *(who was also called Mark)* left the missionary journey at this point, but this one detail ends up playing a much bigger role in the future ministry of Paul, Barnabas, and Mark. For the full story, cross-reference to Acts 15:37-38, Colossians 4:10 and 2 Timothy 4:11.

13:14-52 We see a pattern forming, and it's one that Paul continues throughout his ministry. Upon arriving in a new city, Paul would enter the synagogues to share the gospel. Due to jealousy and disbelief, God's chosen people, the Jews, would largely reject him and the message of the gospel. But no matter how many times it happened, Paul didn't stop starting with the church and keeping church as a crucial aspect of the Christian faith in his teaching and writing. Church and church people were not perfect then, and they're not perfect now. But the church is still described as Christ's bride *(cross-reference to Ephesians 5:21-27)*, so despite imperfection, church is still God's Plan A for gospel community.

13:16-41 Paul first establishes common ground. To the Jewish crowd, he begins with the Old Testament, and then he shares about Jesus. He's working to build trust with them and show the big picture of God's plan that included Jesus from the beginning. It's also a full circle moment, as we see Paul preaching a very similar sermon to the one Stephen preached before he was martyred *(Refer back to commentary for Acts 7)*. Ultimately, Stephen lost his life, but even though it didn't seem that way in the moment, his message did not fall on deaf ears to the young man who held the coats of the men who killed him. Say what God gives you when He gives it to you, no matter the cost. God will use what is done for Him in ways beyond our comprehension.

13:16; 26;38 If there is one notable difference between the sermons of Stephen and Paul, Stephen repeatedly pointed back to Israel's history of rejecting the prophets God sent. Paul continuously extends grace in how he addresses the Jews, referring to them as *"brothers"* and *"you who fear God"* and *"sons of the family of Abraham."* Rather than emphasizing Israel's rejection, Paul emphasizes God's grace in sending the prophets to Israel. By his words, it's not hard to see God's grace is fresh for Paul. As believers, we have experienced God's grace, so we should also extend God's grace to others.

13:30-31 The resurrection truly changes everything. Christ conquering death points to God's ability to grant eternal life to all who believe in Jesus.

13:33 Cross-reference to Psalm 2:7.

13:34 Cross-reference to Isaiah 55:3.

13:35   Cross-reference to Psalm 16:10.

13:36   This phrase should be the goal of every believer: to die *"after [he] had served the purpose of God in [his] own generation."* God calls us to serve Him in ministries for a particular time and for specific people.

13:38-39 The law cannot save us. Jesus can. This does not mean that the law doesn't have a place. But instead of the law being there to save us, the law is there to reveal our sin and our need for a Savior, as well as how to live for the glory of God and the good of others. The law is good, but alone, it cannot give us a relationship with Jesus.

13:41   Cross-reference to Habakkuk 1:5.

13:42   Paul was faithful to share the gospel. It was not a new sermon, and the people begged to hear more. As you teach others, do not fall victim to the belief that people want to hear something new. More than anything new, people need to be reminded of what's true. Never get far away from the gospel as you teach. Saved and unsaved alike, the gospel is truly what we need to hear.

13:43   Urge the people you teach *"to continue in the grace of God"* as Paul and Barnabas did. They won't always get it perfectly, but God's grace will always be there to guide them and show them the way.

13:43   A subtle turning point has occurred here. Luke was likely writing the book of Acts in real time, and the spotlight begins to shift from Barnabas to Paul. Up until this point, when Paul and Barnabas were mentioned together, Barnabas was mentioned first. But as they stepped more and more into Gentile territory, Paul was the one speaking and leading more than Barnabas. In the Kingdom, we can't worry about who gets more attention. Barnabas was willing to mentor someone who ended up outshining him, and we're all better because of it. When you serve in ministry, lay your ego aside. If you hold onto your ego, it will get in the way of the work.

13:35 Once again, jealousy has escalated into more sin, not only by criticizing Paul, but by contradicting what he said (much of which they believed as Jews!). Refuse to view jealousy as a "small" sin, especially when referring to the work God is doing. Celebrate all Kingdom work, and cut off jealousy before it escalates into further destruction.

13:47 Cross-reference to Isaiah 49:6.

13:48-49 No amount of jealousy or disbelief could stop the movement of God then, and the gospel cannot be stopped now either. Continue spreading the word of God, trusting God fully for the results.

13:50 Each of us have influence, but as happens here, having influence doesn't mean you will always use your influence for good. The devout women of high standing and the leading men of the city all used their influence to drive Paul and Barnabas out of the city. One way or the other, you will use your influence. Aim to exclusively use it for good.

13:51 Shaking the dust from your feet was Jewish custom if they walked through Gentile territory. Now, since the Gentiles are included in the gospel, rather than shaking the dust off from the Gentile territory, it was done for anyone who rejected the gospel - including the Jews.

13:52 You are not responsible when others reject God. You are called to faithfully share His message. So although they wanted all of the Jews to accept the gospel and believe in Jesus, they kept their joy in the gospel alone, not in the success of their ministry or in how others responded. It's a heavy world, and not everyone will accept God's message. But despite how others respond, we can keep our joy because of how God responds to us.

Acts 12-13

QUESTIONS

Icebreaker: Adding some humor to an incredible miracle, Rhoda is so shocked to see Peter at Mary's house that she forgets to open the gate and let Peter in. She's too excited to let everyone know God has answered their prayers for Peter! Has there been a time in your life when you prayed for God to move, and you were still so surprised when He showed up that you didn't know what to do? Tell us about it.

1. Read Acts 12:3 aloud. What does this verse say motivated Herod to arrest Peter? Why do you think Herod was motivated to please the Jews? When pleasing people pops up in your life, do you typically find it's somehow rooted in selfishness? Why or why not?

2. James was killed, and God chose to rescue Peter from prison. Seeing the outcome of these two apostles' lives recorded so closely together is a powerful reminder that our circumstances do not dictate God's love for us. God loved both James and Peter. In the tough moments that you do not understand, how can you remind yourself that you can always trust God, and no matter what, you can always be confident He loves you?

3. The days of Unleavened Bread were considered holy, so Herod had Peter arrested but not immediately executed because an execution during these days, according to rules and custom, would have defiled the holy celebration. Do you think this is a trap that we fall into today – seeing certain days or actions as holy instead of simply seeing God as holy? What are some ways this trap presents itself today, and how do we work to not fall into it?

4. I love that Luke takes the time to give us a peak of the diversity of the people of the church at Antioch. But because they had Jesus in common, they could worship, fast, and pray together. D.A. Carson put it this way: *"What binds us together is not common education, common race, common income levels, common politics, common nationality, common accents, common jobs or anything else of that*

sort. Christians come together because they have all been loved by Jesus Himself. They are a band of natural enemies who love one another for Jesus' sake." When you look at the people you are in gospel community with, do you think those on the outside can easily see Jesus as the sole source of your unity, or do other things you have in common compete for their attention instead? What are some practical ways we can prioritize unifying with other believers over Jesus alone? Why is this so important to the watching world around us?

5. God's chosen people, the Jews, largely rejected Paul and the message of the gospel. But no matter how many times it happened, Paul didn't stop starting with the church and keeping church as a crucial aspect of the Christian faith in his teaching and writing. Church and church people were not perfect then, and they're not perfect now. Read Ephesians 5:21-27 as a group. How does the analogy of the church as Christ's bride help us to see that despite imperfection, church is still God's Plan A for gospel community? How do we navigate this conversation with those who have been hurt by the church?

6. Read Acts 13:50 aloud. Each of us has influence, but as we see here, having influence doesn't automatically mean you will always use your influence for good. One way or the other, you will use your influence. How should we think about our influence to help us use it exclusively for good?

7. There are many parallels between the sermon Paul gives in Acts 13 to the one Stephen delivered in Acts 7 before he was martyred. Stephen had no way of knowing the man who held the coats of those who threw stones at him would end up being one of the greatest missionaries of all time. How does that example help you see how God is working even when you can't see what He's doing? Is there anything in your life right now where it's hard to see God is working that we can pray together about?

Acts 14-15

COMMENTARY

14:2-3 Despite great opposition, Paul and Barnabas stayed in Iconium for a long time, preaching and performing miracles. Opposition does not always mean that you should leave. Don't quit because it gets hard. Quit because God tells you it's time to move on.

14:4 Not even miracles could convince some that the gospel was true. Remember that "convincing" others to believe in Jesus is not your job. The Holy Spirit will do all the convincing. You just have to be bold enough to share His truth with great love.

14:7 They moved to a new place, but they continued the same mission. They didn't quit in Iconium because it got hard. They left Iconium so the mission could continue.

14:9 *"Seeing that he had faith to be made well"* is a beautiful phrase that reminds us that while faith is *"the assurance of things hoped for, the conviction of things not seen"* (Hebrews 11:1), our faith is still something that others have the ability to see in us; just as Paul saw the faith of the man who could not use his feet. Put your faith on display. You never know how God will use the moments when others are able to see your faith.

14:11-13 Because the people would have spoken in their Lycaonian language, Paul and Barnabas likely didn't know what was happening in vs. 11 when the people began comparing them to the gods of Roman mythology. It was when the people began to show signs of offering a sacrifice that they likely realized what the crowd was doing and saying.

14:14 Tearing your garments was a sign of grief. Paul and Barnabas didn't simply want to stop the crowd from worshiping them. They were genuinely grieved that the people wanted to give them credit for what God had done. When someone tries to give you credit for God's work, does it grieve you? Even if God uses us to share about Him with others, that does not condone any special treatment. God is the gift.

14:14-18 Look how eager Paul and Barnabas are to share God. They rushed out into the crowd. Their grief didn't push them to feel like they failed and then to give up. Their grief moved them to compassion and filled them with an urgency to try and share the gospel again.

14:15 Because they compared Barnabas to Zeus and Paul to Hermes, they knew the current beliefs of the people in Lystra centered around believing in many gods. It was important for them to begin with creation and show that one God created everything.

14:16-17 Cross-reference to Romans 1:20. Nature itself is enough evidence for God. Take time to look around you when you are outdoors to see the masterpiece God created. Reflect on things like weather, seasons, and even the transition from day to night. It doesn't just randomly occur. The world really does cry out with proof for our great God. Everything we enjoy reflects His existence and goodness.

14:18 Despite your best efforts, people may still give you credit for what God does through you. Their actions reflect their faith that they cannot see past what is seen. You are not responsible for their faith, but you are responsible for yours.

14:19 The same crowd that was convinced Paul was a god days before was now convinced to stone him. Human opinion is so fickle. We cannot allow ourselves to get caught up in what others think of us because what they think now could just as easily change. Cross-reference to John 2:24-25.

14:20-21 Not only is it a miracle that Paul is alive, but let's not miss that he went back into the city where he was stoned and presumed dead *(Lystra)* to resume preaching the gospel. The Great Commandment *(Mark 12:30-31)* of loving God and loving others is not always easy, but powerful examples like this remind us that it's always possible.

14:22-23 If you were to look at their route on a map, you'd be able to see they didn't take the most efficient route. They went out of their way (and traveled back through cities where they had been previously run out of!) because maintaining contact with the believers was more important than their convenience or their comfort. They had five main goals in their visit: 1) to strengthen the believers' souls with the truth of the gospel; 2) to encourage *(literally "to put courage in")* the believers to keep pursuing their faith; 3) to remind them that suffering and hardship are promised, but so is heaven; 4) to appoint elders so there were people there to take responsibility for the church; 5) pray and fast to commit them to the Lord.

14:27 Celebrate what God has done. Recognize the doors He opens and the work He has accomplished. The work should inspire worship, and the worship should inspire the work.

14:28 Paul and Barnabas both followed the command to be Christ's witnesses where He was not known *(Acts 1:8)*, and they also came together with other believers. Our lives should reflect both commands - both to *gather* together with other believers and to *go* and make disciples.

15:1-21 Pursuing unity is extremely important for us as believers. But the pursuit of unity does not mean that there will not be disagreement. The pursuit of unity simply means that when there is disagreement among believers, there should not be division. There are three principles we can gather from the Jerusalem Council to let us know how we should handle conflict among believers: 1) *No one ignored the false doctrine that was being taught.* The problem was addressed. Problems must be faced to be fixed. 2) *Allow all sides of the argument to have a fair hearing.* Sometimes, people bury themselves further into their opinions simply when they do not have an opportunity to be heard. 3) *Hold the discussion in front of a group of spiritually mature leaders.* This discussion took place in front of apostles and elders (vs. 6).

15:1-2 Essentially, these men were saying that in order to be saved, you had to become a Jew first. It was worth having *"no small dissension"* over, as Luke described it, because this was a salvation issue. Any belief that claims there are additional requirements for salvation in addition to Jesus isn't adding to the gospel; it's another gospel altogether. Salvation issues are primary and worth a disagreement. All other non-salvation issues are secondary, and should be treated as such.

15:3 Paul and Barnabas were traveling to Jerusalem for the council meeting to discuss this important issue, but they were more focused on the joy they got from the Gentiles' salvation than on the upcoming argument. If a theological disagreement ever becomes your primary focus above salvation or if you become so focused on defending your position that you no longer have joy in the salvation of others, you've likely made an idol of theological doctrine.

15:4 Even in disagreements, remember what you have in common. Before they discussed the issue at hand, they welcomed one another and celebrated all that God had done.

15:5 The Jews had a lot of traditions, and it was a struggle for many to distinguish between truth and tradition. Transparently, the same struggle still exists in the church today. As we navigate through matters of truth and tradition, our guiding principle must be that no matter how much we may enjoy our traditions, they should never hold the same weight as Jesus. That's an easy way to tell when a tradition has become more of a hindrance than a help.

15:6 Disagreements can be best settled when you bring a group of mature believers together. It's also probably an easy way to know if an argument is worth having in the first place. If you don't want to take the time to consult mature believers on the matter, is the argument worth it?

15:7 *"After there had been much debate,"* implies that everyone gathered had a chance to be heard. In order to have a disagreement in a way that honors the Lord, you must be willing to listen as much as you speak. Don't just listen to respond, but actually listen to what the other person is saying.

15:7-11 In the Kingdom of God, God puts us in different places to be able to be His witnesses. Even in the specific work you may not be called to personally, you can still defend the Kingdom work God has called others to do, just as Peter jumped in to defend the Gentile mission.

15:9 Peter once again acknowledges that Jesus made a way for all to come to God. Although the Jews have once been God's chosen people, Jesus has now made salvation available to all. Faith in Jesus is how we all stand rightly before the Lord.

15:10-11 The law is there to guide us, but it cannot save us. Because none of us could obey the law perfectly, God sent Jesus in our place. Peter reiterates that even though Jews may have kept the law the best they could, we are all saved through the grace of Jesus alone.

15:12 Leaders were speaking at the meeting, but this verse shows us that the whole church was also present. However, this was still a debate happening privately inside the church among believers, not in a public place in front of a mixed audience. Because of social media, it's very easy for believers to disagree in public, both confusing believers and nonbelievers alike. When you disagree with other believers, there is a dual responsibility to both have other believers present and to be diligent to keep these disagreements out of public forums and off public channels.

15:12 Barnabas and Paul backed their position by showing how God was moving among the Gentiles. When we are looking to discern between a disagreement, don't simply follow human logic, but follow where God is moving.

15:13 James speaking here is the half-brother of Jesus who first believed after the resurrection and became a leader in the church at Jerusalem. Consider that as an apologetic to defend Jesus as the Son of God: *what would it take for you to be convinced that your sibling was the promised Messiah?* Jesus' resurrection didn't just convince strangers that Jesus was the Son of God; it convinced His own brother.

15:13-17 James wasn't aiming to merely win the disagreement with his experience, but went to God's Word for truth. As much as you can, settle disagreements with God's Word as the final say.

15:16-17 Cross-reference to Amos 9:10-11.

15:19-21 The Council comes up with four things to help teach the Gentiles both to preserve unity among all believers and to reaffirm the moral law of the Old Testament: 1) to abstain from things polluted by idols *(which had more to do with idolatry than the food)*; 2) to abstain from sexual immorality; 3) to abstain from what had been strangled and 4) to abstain from blood. The Old Testament law consists of three main categories: ceremonial law, civil law, and moral law. The ceremonial law was fulfilled once and for all through Jesus being the sacrifice for our sins, so it no longer applies to us today. And though Jesus perfectly fulfilled the moral law and civil law as well, these laws remain helpful in guiding us to live the gospel in our everyday lives as we aim to love God and love others.

15:22 The disagreement did not divide the believers. They reached a joint decision, and though they all came to the council with different opinions, they left the council with a unified practice moving forward.

15:28 All who wrote the letter were confident the Holy Spirit had guided their discussion and decision. This is a good check for all of us when we present ideas to others: *would this seem good to the Holy Spirit, or does this just seem good to us?*

15:28 The refusal to lay on the Gentiles *"no greater burden than these requirements"* is such a beautiful reminder that our faith is so much more about what Jesus has done than what we do. Yes, truly understanding the gospel will generate a real response from us, but Jesus lifted the greatest burden. To act any other way does not truly reflect the grace of the gospel. These four points did not have any bearing on a person's salvation, but the council recognized that abiding by these guidelines would be helpful for the gospel mission overall.

15:31 When you come together with other believers in unity, especially when there are differences among you, it will result in rejoicing. You don't just have to endure relationships where there is disagreement; you can be greatly encouraged because Jesus covers all of our differences.

15:32   Words are powerful. Use yours to encourage and strengthen others.

15:36-38 In Acts 13:13, we learn that Mark left in the middle of the first missionary journey. Barnabas, being the one who was the first to take a chance on Paul, was ready to give Mark another shot at being their ministry partner. Paul, however, did not want the mission to be held back and was unwilling to take a risk on Mark.

15:39-40 God worked for His glory through their disagreement. With Barnabas taking Mark and Paul choosing Silas, there were now two missionary journeys instead of just one. Because we know how the story ends, that Mark ended up being a valuable ministry partner for Paul *(cross-reference to Colossians 4:10; 2 Timothy 4:11)* and that Mark ended up writing the first gospel account, the Gospel of Mark, it's easy to credit Barnabas for Mark's successful ministry. And while I'm sure Barnabas' encouragement definitely contributed to Mark's ministry, because we know Mark and Paul reconciled, it's also plausible that Paul's rebuke impacted Mark positively too. While we don't know exactly who to credit most for impacting Mark to finish well, the best possible guess is that it was probably a combination of Barnabas' kindness and Paul's rebuke. It's a good reminder for us that we can never take matters of people lightly, and we must always obey God, even if God calls us to have a different role in a person's life than He asks of another believer.

15:40   Paul and Silas were on opposite sides of the Jerusalem Council, and now, they're ministry partners. Paul taking Silas with him is another way to see that the unity after this decision wasn't just for show, but it was real. Unity takes work. Make efforts to pursue unity with believers who are different from you.

15:41   *"Strengthening the churches"* is a special phrase to our ministry at She Works His Way, because it's one of our mission principles that guides our decisions. We wholeheartedly believe that the local church is God's Plan A for evangelism and discipleship. Therefore, as we make decisions for our para-church ministry, we aim that everything we do strengthen the church as a whole and not merely benefit the SWHW ministry.

Acts 14-15

QUESTIONS

Icebreaker: Despite great opposition, Paul and Barnabas stayed in Iconium for a long time, preaching and performing miracles. Have you ever stayed in a situation when it was really hard because God was still moving? Tell us what you saw God do because you refused to quit when it was difficult.

1. Read Acts 14:9-10 aloud. How do you think Paul was able to see this man *"had faith to be made well?"* What are ways that you can live in such a way that others see your faith? (Have another group member read Hebrews 11:1 aloud to remember how Scripture defines faith for us.)

2. Read Acts 14:16-17 aloud as well as Romans 1:20. How do you see nature itself as being evidence for God? As a group, reflect on things like weather, seasons, and even the transition from day to night and how they do not just randomly occur. The world really does cry out with proof for our great God. Everything we enjoy reflects His existence and goodness. What aspects of creation leave you in awe of God?

3. Read Acts 14:22-23 aloud. What were the five main goals Paul and Barnabas had when they visited the churches they established? How can we prioritize the same five things when we gather together as believers today?

4. Paul and Barnabas took seriously the commands to go and make disciples as well as to gather together with other believers. We are called to both - not one or the other. Which command is easier for you to obey – to go and make disciples or to gather together with other believers? What can you do to obey more in the area where you are weaker?

5. There's so much wisdom for us to glean from how the believers handled the disagreement that ultimately led to the Jerusalem Council. A few questions to discuss as a group: 1) Since we are called to unity, what made this issue worth a disagreement? How would you define the difference between a salvation issue and a secondary issue? What can we learn about how the church leaders handled this disagreement that would still be valuable for us to practice today as we experience conflict and disagreement with other believers?

6. Jesus' resurrection didn't just convince strangers that Jesus was the Son of God, but it convinced His own brother. How does that increase your confidence that Jesus really is the Son of God? *(Think about it: what would it take for your sibling to convince you that he/she was God's child?)*

7. God worked for His glory through the disagreement between Paul and Barnabas. With Barnabas taking Mark and Paul choosing Silas, there were now two missionary journeys instead of just one. Instead of being selfish and allowing their differences in opinion to make them bitter and divide them, all four men kept their focus on the main mission of spreading the gospel. How do you surrender your personal feelings for another and make sure you follow the Holy Spirit's prompting in obedience?

Acts 16-17

COMMENTARY

16:1 In his 2nd letter to Timothy, Paul expands on the faith of Timothy's mother and grandmother. Cross-reference to 2 Timothy 1:5.

16:3 Because Timothy grew up in the area where they were ministering, people knew his father was a Greek. Paul had Timothy get circumcised because he didn't want to waste energy on nonessentials of faith. Paul, like Timothy, grew up Jewish. He wasn't opposed to anything of Jewish tradition, like circumcision, except for the instances, like the Jerusalem Council, where people were adding to what was required for salvation. This is not people-pleasing or conforming to expectations, but removing obstacles so they could minister to people more effectively without distraction.

16:5 Luke frequently chronicles the growth of the church in Acts, but it's never simply about the numbers. Here, he notes how churches were strengthened in the faith, and because of their strengthened faith, they grew. Make strengthened faith the goal and trust God for numerical growth.

16:6-7 The Holy Spirit will guide you in what to do and what *not* to do. And it's not merely a matter of doing something right or doing something wrong, but the Holy Spirit can and will guide each of us personally. Here, Paul and Silas were forbidden and stopped by the Holy Spirit from going to certain cities to preach the gospel. It's not that preaching the gospel in those cities would have been wrong, but God had other plans for them of where He needed them to go. Pay attention to His guidance.

16:9-10 The vision was brief of a man asking for help in Macedonia, and they interpreted it to mean they needed to take the gospel to Macedonia. As you help others, remember that the gospel is what both saves us and sustains us.

16:10 The pronouns *"we"* and *"us"* used here indicate that this was when Luke joined Paul on his second missionary journey.

16:13 It took 10 men to make a Jewish synagogue in a city, so that means in this area, there were less than 10 Jewish men since there was a place of prayer but no synagogue. They still stuck to their normal routine as best they could by going to the place of prayer to connect with people who were interested in spiritual matters.

Also note that cultural boundaries would have prevented men and women from speaking to one another in public. However, just as Paul didn't let the cultural differences and subsequent boundaries stop him from sharing the gospel here, we shouldn't let them get in our way either.

16:14 God opened Lydia's heart to pay attention to Paul's words and to respond. Salvation is the supernatural work of God, not the persuasiveness or eloquence of the preacher. When you share the gospel, remember that it's not as much about your words or gift of speaking as it is about God's work in hearts.

16:15 It's not uncommon in the book of Acts to record that a person was saved along with their whole household. Even when an entire family is converted and shared as a unit, salvation is an individual decision. Lydia's conversion and baptism, along with the conversions and baptisms of her household, indicates that she shared the gospel with her family after she got saved.

16:15 Lydia blessed the apostles and the church with her gift of hospitality. [Acts 16:40 indicates that Lydia's home became the gathering place for the believers.] Open your home to others. The root word for hospitality in the Greek is the same as the word "hospital." In our world today, we tend to confuse hospitality with entertaining. Hospitality is about the guest, but entertaining usually makes the gathering about the host. Remove all of the Pinterest boards from your mind on what it means to be a hostess, and see your home more like a hospital instead. Is your home a place where hurting people can come and feel better when they leave?

16:16 The slave girl with *"a spirit of divination"* is another way to say this slave girl had a demonic spirit. She was a demon-possessed child, and instead of helping her, her owners were exploiting her pain for their own gain.

16:17 It's so interesting to think that the demons recognized Jesus as the Son of God, and yet, so many of the religious leaders did not.

16:18 Why was Paul greatly annoyed? Though her words were true, he probably did not want anyone to mis-associate her as being his ministry partner. Perhaps he was just righteously indignant that truth and evil do not mix. Or maybe because she kept saying the same phrase over and over for several days, he's finally just had enough.

16:18 Cross-reference to Matthew 8:16, Matthew 10:8, Matthew 12:28, and Luke 10:17. Jesus exercised His authority over demons while He was on earth, and He gave the same authority to His disciples as well. Rather than praying to God, Paul spoke directly to the demon and commanded it to come out in the name of Jesus. Paul's power or authority did not make the demon come out; the power and authority of Jesus did.

16:19 When money becomes a motivator, it often works against the gospel. We saw it already with the magician *(Acts 8:18-24)*, we see it here, and we'll see it again with the silversmith *(Acts 19:24)*. When profit matters more than God's glory, salvation, or what's best for others, money has become an idol.

16:19-24 Paul and Silas were falsely accused, stripped, beaten, and imprisoned without a fair hearing. Do not expect to be treated fairly when you live for Jesus. Expect increased opposition more than you expect fairness.

16:25 After being stripped, beaten, and imprisoned, Paul and Silas chose to praise God, and the prisoners paid attention. When your praise for God follows hardship, that's likely to be the time that most people will listen to you.

16:26-27 Prison guards who lost their prisoners were typically given the same sentence as the prisoner they lost. The jailer supposed that because he lost all of the prisoners, he was going to be killed anyway. The thing that I find the most intriguing in this miracle is not merely that Paul and Silas didn't escape, but that none of the other prisoners tried to escape either. This side of heaven, we'll never know why, but my best guess is that the prisoners were so curious about Paul and Silas' faith on display through their worship that they stayed to see what would happen next.

16:28-29 Just like people will listen if you praise God after hardship, they will also likely be curious about God if you care about someone who has treated you poorly. There's a good chance the jailer who is with them was also one of the men who beat them.

16:30 You never know who is listening to you or watching you. But because the jailer's question was about how he could be saved, we know he was listening to Paul and Silas' teaching or their worship.

16:31 Notice they told him to "believe *in*" the Lord Jesus, and not just to "believe *that*" the Lord Jesus... There is a difference between believing *in* Jesus and believing *that* Jesus. Put your full confidence in Jesus.

16:32-33 God can change people through the gospel. Hours before, the jailer inflicted wounds upon Paul and Silas. And now that he has learned of Christ, the jailer is washing their wounds. No one is too far gone for God to reach.

16:34 Joy and salvation go together. When you find yourself fighting for joy, recall the gospel. Remember what Jesus did for you. Reflect on your life before Christ and your life now. Our salvation should lead us to rejoice!

16:35-39 Paul is not trying to get justice for the way they were treated, but he is trying to make sure that their release is as public as their arrest. He didn't want others to falsely believe that Christianity was a threat to Rome, as they were accused. Paul wanted it to be clear a mistake was made to protect the future of the gospel and the witness of Christ. He is standing up for others who could be in their situation in the future.

16:40 Although they were probably physically sore from their beating and exhausted from not sleeping in prison, they prioritized making time to encourage the church at Philippi. The next time you read Philippians, do so picturing some of the people we've met, that Paul would have been writing to, like Lydia and the jailer.

17:1-3 Twice in this chapter *(vs. 2 and vs. 17)*, Luke uses the word *"reasoned"* to describe Paul's teaching. Paul wasn't looking for an argument or looking to get them to make a decision without engaging their minds. To reason with someone is to think through logically while allowing them to do the same. It's a patient persuasion. Just as the text says here, Scripture is our explanation and our proof, so we don't have to approach these conversations like we're trying to start conflict or convince.

17:2 Even though Old Testament references were clear that the coming Messiah would suffer, some Jews resisted this message. Cross-reference to Psalm 22, Isaiah 53, Zechariah 12:10, Zechariah 13:7.

17:4-5 In drastic contrast with Paul's approach of reasoning over Scripture, the Jews revolted against Paul and Silas, not in theological debate, but simply over jealousy.

17:6 Though it was said in a negative way, the truth is that the gospel *should* always be rocking the world, turning it upside down. The gospel is drastically different from every other religion in that it hinges upon what Jesus has done versus what a person must do. We shouldn't be able to be quiet about it or pretend like it doesn't affect every area of our lives. How does the gospel turn your world upside down in the best way?

17:7-8 Paul didn't disparage the government any time he preached. He did elevate Jesus and the gospel, but he did so without tearing anyone or any other institution down. These were false claims made by his accusers because they knew that Paul's message alone would probably not be enough for punishment. However, they knew speaking poorly of Caesar or Rome would be taken seriously.

17:9   Jason and those who were arrested posted bond for their freedom by insisting Paul and Silas would not stir up any more trouble. Because they put money down as security, if trouble continued, Jason and the others could have lost their money, property, or even their lives. There's a good chance this is what Paul referred to as *"Satan's hindrance"* in 1 Thessalonians 2:18.

17:11   Describing these Jews as more *"noble"* than the ones in Thessalonica did not mean that they were more educated or prestigious. In fact, Thessalonica was one of the wealthiest and influential cities Paul visited. But rather, Luke is saying these Jews were more open-minded and fair in the reasoning of the Scriptures.

17:11-12 These verses give us some valuable insight on how we should approach Scripture and conversations about the Bible: 1) We should be eager to hear from the Lord. 2) We should compare what we hear with what God's Word says. 3) We need to seek His Word daily. 4) We can believe what we read. Study and examine Scripture, and ask the Holy Spirit to help you understand.

17:14-15 Since Paul was the main spokesperson in Thessalonica and the one who angered them the most, they sent Paul off immediately, but Silas and Timothy stayed in Berea until Paul sent for them when he arrived in Athens. I'm sure it would have been easier and even more enjoyable for them to consistently travel together, but this is yet another example of how they put the mission ahead of their preferences.

17:16   Seeing that the city was full of idols let Paul know that many around him were lost. I love the phrase *"his spirit was provoked within him."* It should provoke our spirit when we see that others around us are lost. It should stir us to prayer and to beg God to intervene. It should lead us to courage, asking God to use us in any way He wishes to share the gospel and to point others to the truth. It should also stir up compassion, desiring for them to come to a saving knowledge of Jesus Christ, just as we have. We shouldn't be able to come in contact with a lost world and be unbothered.

17:17 Paul ministered in two main places in Athens: the synagogue and the marketplace. Our lives can and should look very similar. We should be part of the body of Christ, the local church. And wherever our marketplace is, where we find ourselves many hours of our days, we should find ways to minister there too. The workplace is probably the most underutilized mission field that Christians occupy daily. What kind of difference would it make if every believer showed up to their work primarily to be God's witness?

17:18 The Epicurean philosophers believed life's goal is pleasure and happiness. Very similar to the new age movement we see today, their beliefs centered around, "If it feels good, it is good." The Stoic philosophers were very different in their beliefs, being highly disciplined, and valued the intellectual over the emotional. They believed thinking was far superior to feeling. Similar to agnostic and atheist beliefs today, the Stoics believed that life is meaningless, that it simply is what it is.

17:19-21 Despite the philosophical differences between the two groups, both groups were very open-minded about learning new things and wanted to hear Paul's message. Something to our advantage as we evangelize in the world today that is very similar to the people of Athens: most people are open-minded to "spiritual" conversations.

17:22-31 If there was an outline for how to present the gospel at work, this is it. This is Paul's marketplace sermon. Paul is speaking these words in the middle of the marketplace, not in the middle of a synagogue. He tailors his message to match the tone and the needs of the audience, but he doesn't veer from truth.

17:22 Paul begins by focusing on the positive and what they have in common: *"I see that you are very religious."* When you are beginning spiritual conversations with those who do not know the Lord, be quick to be kind.

17:23 Instead of judging them for worshiping idols, Paul took what they already believed and helped them see God as the answer they were looking for and that he knew the one they worshiped as the *"unknown God."*

17:24-25 Paul took what they had already experienced of God in creation and aimed to enlarge their vision of who God is. I've been surprised in many conversations I've had with people that I thought didn't have any belief in God who agree it's hard to imagine how the world came to be without a Creator.

17:26-27 Knowing his audience is vastly different in their beliefs on intellect and emotion, Paul speaks to both groups. *"They should seek God"* emphasizes intellect and *"feel their way toward Him and find Him"* hints toward the emotion of hope that there is a God to find and it's not hard to find Him.

17:28 The two quotes we see here are not quotes from the Old Testament, but quotes from their own poets and mythology. Paul is not condoning these beliefs, but rather, he's aiming to show them that some of their current beliefs are already hints toward faith. As we examine the beliefs in our world today, many of them are not brand new beliefs, but they are simply twisted versions of God's truth. Probably the most popular beliefs today simply replace a theology of God with a theology of "me." As you are looking to decipher through these beliefs yourself, one of the easiest ways to spot a flawed gospel is one that points more to self than it points to God.

17:29 As Paul gently moves toward the errors in their current beliefs, he uses *"we"* language, acknowledging himself as a sinful human, rather than simply pointing fingers at the people of Athens. It's critical that we share the gospel from a posture of humility, that recognizes we were once lost too. Every time you share the gospel, it's a reminder of what Jesus saved you from, not just a hope He will save someone else.

17:30-31 Paul does not separate the call to repentance from the hope of Christ. Because Jesus entered the world and conquered sin and death, we are called to repent and believe in Him. The proof that we will be able to have eternal life through Jesus is because of Christ's resurrection. When you share the gospel, we do have to recognize our own sin and that there's no way we could get to heaven on our own merit, but we also get to rest in the hope that Christ's work on the cross is final, forever and finished. Dwell on the hope that we have in Jesus more than the sin that separates us because you know how the story ends.

17:32-34 There were three responses from the crowd in Athens that are still the responses we can expect when we share the gospel today: 1) Some mocked. 2) Some wanted to know more. 3) Some believed. Remember that your job is obedience to share, not how others respond to God's message. God is the one who moves in and changes hearts. Be bold when He calls you to share, and trust Him to do the rest.

Acts 16-17

QUESTIONS

Icebreaker: In Chapter 16, we learn about Lydia who is known for her hospitality. Let's face it, some of us are naturally good at this, and others of us have to work a little harder. But remember, hospitality isn't about being good at entertaining people; it's about being good at making people feel seen and loved. Having said that, if a group of us were going to come over to your house tonight, what would you serve and what would our activity be? *(This is hypothetical, so there are no rules. Catering is allowed, and there is no budget!)*

1. Even though Paul and Silas were stripped, beaten, and placed in prison, they "were praying and singing hymns to God" *(Acts 16:25).* Can you think of a time in your life when things around you seemed like they were falling apart, but inside you had perfect peace from the Lord? Tell us about it. Do you find that more people were curious about your faith during your trials than they are in the times when your life is easier? Why or why not?

2. Read Acts 16:28 aloud. What do Paul's words reveal, not only about himself, but about all of the other prisoners? Why do you think the other prisoners stayed when the earthquake provided them a way to escape? What does that remind us about the unbelievers around us?

3. It's easy to gloss over the beauty in Acts 16:33: the difference the gospel made in the jailer's life was that he went from inflicting wounds to washing their wounds. There's no change too subtle to praise God for, but the truth is that the gospel changes us. What do you think is one of the biggest changes in your life that you or others may notice about you since you understood the gospel?

4. Read Acts 17:2-3 as well as Acts 17:11-12. These verses provide great insight for how we should approach Scripture for ourselves and with others. What truth from these verses stands out to you most for how you should view and interact with God's Word?

5. Read Acts 17:16. Seeing that the city was full of idols let Paul know that many around him were lost. What do you think it meant that Paul's *"spirit was provoked?"* When we are reminded of the lost world, should it provoke our spirit too? How do we remain aware of the lost people around us?

6. Paul's sermon in the marketplace is the closest thing to an outline we'll ever get for how to share the gospel in secular places. What does Paul say in these verses that equips you to know how to engage in spiritual conversations with those around you? What can we learn from his words and use in our conversations today?

7. I love that as Paul transitions to the errors in their beliefs (17:29) that he begins using *"we"* language instead of *"you"* language. It's critical that we share the gospel from a posture of humility that recognizes we were once lost too. Every time we share the gospel, it's a reminder of what Jesus saved us from, not just a hope He will save someone else. When you share the gospel with others, what are some things you say? Share some questions you ask or verses you share to equip one another to share the gospel with increased humility and confidence.

Acts 18-20

COMMENTARY

18:1 Corinth was the political and commercial center of Greece.

18:3 Paul was a tent maker by trade. His work was not a means of getting ahead or accumulating wealth. Instead, he used his tent making to provide for his missionary journeys and to connect with others, like Priscilla and Aquila, when he arrived in a new city. Do you view your work in a similar way?

18:5 When you have theological discussions, be *"occupied with the Word,"* as Luke describes Paul. You're much more likely to stay grounded in truth if you let Scripture be your main influence.

18:4-6 Paul was patient to reason and persuade, and after people accepted and believed, he would frequently stay to continue to teach and encourage them. But when the response was unbelief, Paul didn't hold himself accountable for the results. Be faithful to share, but remember you are not responsible for the results.

18:7 Paul may have declared his innocence in the Jews' response to the gospel, but he kept the door open for conversations with them by simply moving his ministry next door.

18:8 The phrase that the Corinthians *"believed and were baptized,"* emphasizes salvation and taking their first step of obedience.

18:9-11 Paul had largely been unable to remain in a place for very long because opposition typically ran him out of town. God was so good to reassure Paul that he would be safe to stay in Corinth. These verses give us a picture of the tension that exists between human responsibility and God's sovereignty in the gospel mission. It was Paul's responsibility to stay and teach in Corinth, and God knew the hearts of the people Paul would minister to there.

The only place where Paul ministered longer than Corinth was Ephesus.

18:12-16 God delivers quickly on His promise to Paul that no one would attack or harm him in Corinth. Gallio's judgment that the accusations of the Jews against Christianity were a religious issue and not a political one set an important precedent that Christians were innocent of breaking Roman law simply by teaching Christian doctrine. A similar ruling is made in Acts 25:19 when Paul appears before Agrippa.

18:18 To learn more about what it means to be *"under a vow,"* cross-reference to Numbers 6:1-21. Typically, Jews would take a vow to express gratitude to God or to seek God's blessing for a future endeavor.

18:19 Don't miss the repetition of Paul's assignment. He came into a new city, he entered a synagogue, and he reasoned with the Jews. Even though the Jews in Corinth rejected him, he continued to pursue the call God put on his life.

18:20-21 Paul's response shows that he is allowing God to direct his steps. To read more from James, Jesus' half-brother, on the phrase *"if the Lord wills,"* cross-reference to James 4:13-17.

18:23 This marks the beginning of Paul's third missionary journey.

18:23 While our assignments may differ from one another, we can all live in such a way that aims to strengthen other disciples of Jesus.

18:24-26 Here's everything we learn about Apollos in these two verses: 1) He is from a cultured city. 2) He knew Scripture well. 3) He had been taught about Jesus. 4) He taught with boldness, passion, and accuracy. 5) He was a gifted communicator. Most Biblical historians agree that Apollos was likely a stronger communicator in spoken word than Paul. 6) His weakness was that he only knew of the baptism of John. This implies that he didn't know of the baptism Jesus instructed after His resurrection *(Matthew 28:19)*. What he knew, he taught well, but there were gaps in what he knew concerning the fullness of what Jesus had commanded. More of the gaps in what Apollos likely taught will be explained in greater detail in Acts 19:1-7.

18:26-28 There's much to learn from the interaction between Priscilla and Aquila with Apollos on both sides. First, they listened to Apollos for themselves. Then, they did not correct him publicly, but instead they privately taught him the pieces of the gospel he did not know. From Apollos, we see that he was humble and teachable. After being instructed by Priscilla and Aquila, he was even more effective in his teaching.

19:1 Ephesus was a Roman province in Asia.

19:1-5 These men had likely been taught by Apollos, as they emphasized the baptism of John as the end of their understanding concerning Jesus. Apollos seemed to know more about Jesus than the men here, but it seemed these men knew *about* Jesus but didn't know Jesus. They were disciples of John the Baptist, but they were not disciples of Jesus. Paul helps them understand that the point of John's ministry was to point others to Jesus, and then they believe and are baptized. As we meet others and discuss spiritual things, what's most important is what they believe about Jesus. Salvation has nothing to do with Biblical knowledge or partial beliefs, but full belief in who Jesus is and what Jesus did.

19:6 Their actions of speaking in tongues and prophesying reflected the inner change that happened with salvation. The same is true for all believers. When the Holy Spirit lives in you, there will be outward changes in behavior that reflect the change Christ has made on the inside.

19:8-9 Again, Paul is faithful to share, but when others begin speaking evil about Christian beliefs, he doesn't engage in the fight. He withdraws. It reminds me of how he lived some of his last words in his letter to Timothy: *"I have fought the good fight"* (2 Timothy 4:7). There will never be a shortage of fights in life. It's important to know the ones that are the good fights and worth fighting as well as knowing the ones that are just fights and worth walking away from.

19:9 The hall of Tyrannus was a school of philosophy. Because many people's jobs required outdoor labor, many didn't work during the hottest hours of the day and would come there to hear Paul teach.

19:10 Ephesus was the longest stay of all of Paul's missionary journeys. In total, he ministered there for about three years.

19:11-12 Even if our hands do the work, God is the one that does the miracle. As he records the growth of the church, Luke is careful to credit God alone, and we should do the same.

19:13-14 The difference between Paul and the seven sons: Paul performed miracles as a way of showing God's power and pointing people to the gospel and the seven sons were attempting to do miracles in the name of Jesus to use Jesus' power for profit and personal gain. This further emphasizes that *"in the name of Jesus"* is not some magical phrase, but that miraculous things can be done in His name with real faith.

19:15 This has to be one of the simultaneously eerie but challenging verses in Scripture. This evil spirit knew Jesus, recognized Paul, but had no idea who these men were who were attempting to use the name of Jesus for their own gain. The flesh part of me doesn't want to be recognized by an evil spirit, but the faith part of me does. It's also just a reminder to us that we don't have access to God's power through another human. Even though these men knew Paul, that didn't give them access to Jesus. Each of us must know Jesus for ourselves.

19:13-16 This is a strange turn of events to see a reverse exorcism of sorts. Normally, the exorcists were the ones who would drive demons out of a human, but here, the demon drove them out of their territory. The demon was able to overpower them because even though they called on the name of Jesus, their faith was not real.

19:18-19 It's easy to gloss over this, discounting fifty thousand pieces of silver to be what we would view as fifty thousand quarters. But fifty thousand pieces of silver then would represent about $6 million today. Destroying these magic books was a way of publicly declaring that they would not go back to their former ways of life and also showed that they held Christ to be their greatest treasure. What are the things that are from your life before Christ that you no longer want to engage in? Do you hang on to these things, or have you worked to destroy them and make sure they have no place in your new life in Christ?

19:20 Instead of just calculating the growth of the church, Luke is noting that the gospel overall is increasing and prevailing. While we each have our own place where we take the gospel and specific work that we are called to, it matters that we see all Kingdom work as a whole too. Celebrate when you see God move, even if it's movements that have nothing to do with you.

19:21 Paul's desire to get to Rome had nothing to do with his personal desire, but his ambition for the gospel. At this time, Rome was the center of the world's influence. If Paul could get the gospel to Rome, the gospel would naturally spread quicker to other regions.

19:23-26 Demetrius, the silversmith, is not opposing the gospel over disbelief, but merely because a huge portion of their business is centered around making idols. He felt the expansion of the gospel threatened his profit margin.

19:27-28 He was honest with his fellow tradesmen about his concern for their industry if making idols were to become a thing of the past, but he also came up with a cover story as an attempt to mask their greed. Instead of leading with fear for their business, he begins cultivating a narrative of loyalty to Artemis, one of the goddesses frequently worshiped as well as an over-the-top sense of patriotism to Ephesus. No one wants to admit to greed, so when thoughts of greed pop up, we often try to cover them up with excuses that sound more noble. Beware of trying to cover your greed.

19:30-31 Paul was the main focus of the riot, so the disciples and his friends were trying to keep him safe. I love that we have this small example of how though Paul was the leader, he practiced mutual submission. Though he wanted to address the crowd and the conflict head-on, he allowed others to speak truth into his life and stayed back from the conflict. It doesn't make you less of a leader if you don't require everyone to do everything your way all of the time. It makes you a trustworthy leader. Have people who can speak truth into your life. We all need it.

19:32 This is the mob mentality in action. Some people showed up and started shouting even though they had no idea what was going on. Today, we don't even have to walk into a crowd to discover the mob. The mob mentality is available to us virtually, literally at our fingertips. This is a good reminder not to just follow the crowd. Before we allow our emotions and actions to take over, we need to stop, hear what's going on, and make sure our feelings, beliefs, and behaviors are informed, not just reactions.

19:33-34 As a Jew, the crowd knew that he opposed other gods. They did not want to allow anyone to speak who wouldn't defend the economic success of Ephesus.

19:35-41 Since Ephesus was a Roman province in Asia, they were under the authority of Rome. An *"unlawful assembly"* could have repercussions for the Ephesian government with the Roman officials. The town clerk diffused the mob, not by settling the argument, but by encouraging them to use the court system to settle the dispute. Over the last several years, Paul has spent a large portion of his ministry proclaiming the gospel inside the synagogues and the marketplace. But coming up, the courts will be one of the primary places God calls Paul to share the gospel.

20:1-2 After a mob nearly started because of his teaching, Paul still gathered the disciples to encourage them before he left Ephesus. He traveled, and he encouraged. He traveled more, and he encouraged more. He had to be tired. After all, the battle between our flesh and spirit is real. But most of the time, if we don't battle our flesh, we don't give our spirit an opportunity to rally. Fight your flesh and give God a chance to show up through you.

20:1 Macedonia is where Philippi is located.

20:3 During these three months is when most Bible historians assume Paul wrote the letter to the Romans.

20:4 It's easy to gloss over all of the names and cities listed here without reflecting on their meaning. Each of these men represented churches Paul helped start in Asia. People are vital to ministry. When we think about what God has called us to, let's remember that many of God's assignments come in people form, not merely projects.

20:7 This is the first reference in Acts to worship taking place on a Sunday.

20:7-9 There were two main factors that contributed to the young boy falling asleep: 1) Paul didn't start speaking until midnight. 2) The lamps here were actually candles in lanterns, so in addition to providing light, they would have made the room warmer.

20:12 Have you noticed how often in his descriptions that instead of saying, "they were very comforted," he says, *"they were not a little comforted"*? Earlier, he has done this by describing circumstances as *"no little disturbance" (Acts 12:18)* and *"they remained no little time with the disciples" (Acts 14:28)*. I'm not certain why Luke chooses to phrase things this way, but I know that it makes me think and weigh his words carefully. Specifically, in this instance, consider the times God shows up, like He did in saving this boy's life. I can't imagine a small reaction... but yet sometimes, in our fast-paced, on-to-the-next-thing world, we probably move on quicker than we should. Maybe instead of being greatly comforted when God shows up, our reaction should be such that someone else would describe it as "not a little" instead.

20:16 Paul decided to sail past Ephesus, not because he didn't love them and didn't want to visit, but because of his love for his friends at a place where he ministered for so long; he knew there would not be a way for it to be a quick trip. Since he missed Passover in Jerusalem, he was trying to get there to celebrate Pentecost. A stop in Ephesus would likely not make his arrival to Jerusalem on time.

20:17-38 This is one of my favorite displays of godly leadership in all of Scripture. Paul's words to his leaders are personal, loving, and truthful. The response of the elders at Ephesus shows how much they truly loved Paul for who he was to them, not just grateful for his words or his teaching. Slow down, read, and re-read. Whether you are someone who believes you are a leader or not, leadership is not a title. Leadership is service. Paul served the church at Ephesus well, and as we serve others, there is much we can glean from the wisdom in these verses.

20:18 His claim that he *"lived among them"* is also a reminder that they know him. They didn't just know *of* Paul, but they really *knew* him. We live in a world where there's no shortage of gospel-centered content. But how much transformation and sanctification are happening when we only hear skillful words coming from a large platform outside the benefit of a personal relationship? Combining truth with an example, **you** are the best person to reach the people around you with the gospel.

20:19 Everything Paul did in Ephesus was serving the Lord. Even when we serve others, we must keep the perspective that we are serving God. Paul lists three things that were required of him to serve the Lord: all humility, tears, and trials.

20:20 Paul was willing to share the whole truth of Scripture, but he didn't waste his time on non-gospel issues. [For more on the difference between profitable and not profitable, cross-reference to 1 Corinthians 10:23-24.] By indicating he taught this way publicly and house to house, he acknowledged that he shared the same convictions to a crowd as he would an individual. It's also important to note that Paul prioritized both public and private teaching. As leadership and influence grow, it's typical for the leader's public activity and private activity to look more and more different. Aim to keep your public and private activity similar. Last, Paul mentions his teaching ministry, but it's mentioned after his personal walk and example. Who you are will ultimately matter more than what you say or do.

20:21 Highlighting that his ministry included both Jews and Greeks is important because Paul's pointing out that he ministered to the Jews who were like him and to the Greeks who were not like him. As you've seen, there's still tension among the Jews about extending the gospel to the Gentiles. Paul is reminding his leaders that the gospel is for everyone, and many times, we need that same reminder. Share the gospel past your comfort zone. And what should you share? Repentance toward God and faith in Jesus. It's simple, and it's enough.

20:22-23 Paul followed the Holy Spirit into Jerusalem even though he likely knew it meant suffering. But he also had peace from the Holy Spirit that it wouldn't be any different going to another city. Wherever he went, opposition and imprisonment would be waiting for him.

20:24 Paul was not worried about what would happen to him or if his life would end. He just wanted to finish well in his ministry of one great task: sharing the gospel.

20:25 Paul is preparing them that they won't see him again. He's not trying to make them sad or scare them. He's making sure they understand that leading the church at Ephesus is now their responsibility.

20:26-27 Paul is confident he can not return to Ephesus, not because the work is done, but because he shared with them everything they need to know to continue the work. He is building their confidence that they can do this without him because they still have what they *really* need: God and His truth.

20:28-29 Paul told them to watch themselves and to watch over the people of the church. As the leaders, these were the men who probably had the most understanding of Scripture. But despite what we know, we are still capable of falling into sin. Don't get so caught up watching over other people that you forget to also watch yourself. Paul warns them equally against evil and ego. When we think about what divides a church, we would typically warn about evil, but there is equal danger in ego. Fight against your pride, or your pride will fight against your Kingdom impact.

20:31 *"Be alert"* reminds them to never coast. I remember my pastor when I was growing up used to say, *"Becoming casual about the gospel is the first step to becoming a casualty."* Paul's also reminding them that it will be hard work, and it will take time. The phrase *"admonish every one with tears"* also shows how much Paul really loved these people, which is why he continued the work day and night for three years. Don't try leading people without loving them.

20:32 Not only is Paul reminding them that they are in God's hands, but he's also probably reminding himself of that truth too. Because he *really* loved them, this speech is not for show. Paul is reminding himself that they are in this work together, even if they're serving apart, but one day, they'll be together again in heaven.

20:33-35 Paul is familiar with the hard work they have ahead of them. He knows that it will be difficult to provide for themselves and to do the work of the ministry, but they've gotten to watch him do it. But Paul doesn't just point to his example to motivate them. He reminds them of Jesus' words.

20:35 *"It is more blessed to give than to receive"* is not recorded in any of the four Gospel accounts, but we assume it was a phrase that was passed down by the disciples that Jesus taught. This is just a reminder that not all of Jesus' earthly life was written down. As amazing as what we know is, there's much more Jesus said and did during His earthly ministry.

20:36 He taught them one last time, but by praying with them, Paul was acknowledging that he knew his words didn't have power, but God does. Godly leadership does not happen without prayer. Pray *for* and pray *with* the people you lead.

20:37 You can't fake this kind of love. There are no shortcuts. Not only did they all cry, but as Paul got on the ship to leave, they went with him. They wanted to be with him every second that they could. Again, the love Paul had for them stretched far beyond merely teaching them. If you do not do life with the people you lead, you cannot expect to leave this kind of impact. It doesn't mean they won't be grateful for what you taught them or the time they had with you, but this kind of love requires more than words or brief interactions. Get in the trenches and really love people. It's what Jesus did for us.

Acts 18-20

QUESTIONS

Icebreaker: We see a lot of repetition in Paul's assignment. I wonder if you ever feel the same in the places where God has called you. I think one of the enemy's greatest schemes is to try and make us feel bored in our calling. Share with us what you do most often that you know God has called you to do, and let's encourage one another to stay the course where God has us.

1. Read Acts 18:4-5. What do you think it means that Paul was *"occupied with the word?"* When you've had theological discussions with others, do you notice a difference when the conversation happens in Scripture vs. out of it? Why do you think that is?

2. Read Acts 18:20-21, then read James 4:13-17. Do you think you approach your life with an *"if the Lord wills"* mindset? What gets in the way of us thinking this way, and how can we take intentional steps to highlight God as the one who directs our steps?

3. Apollos was a gifted teacher, but because he only knew about the baptism of John, there were gaps in what he knew of Christ. What can we learn from the way Priscilla and Aquila corrected Apollos and Apollos' response? What stands out to you from this interaction in Acts 18:26-28?

4. Read Acts 19:13-15. What was the difference between Paul performing miracles *"in the name of Jesus"* and when the Jewish exorcists said the same words? What does the evil spirit's response teach us about what he knew about Jesus? Paul? The men who were attempting to use the name of Jesus for their own gain? How does this challenge you?

5. Read Acts 19:18-19 aloud. But in place of "50 thousand pieces of silver," say today's equivalent amount of $6 million. How does that change the way you hear these words? Since they were worth so much money, what does this teach us about their new commitment to the gospel and how they valued Christ? How can we put the same principle into practice in our own lives? What are the things that are from your life before Christ that you no longer want to engage in? Are you hanging on to them, or have you worked to destroy them and make sure they have no place in your new life in Christ? Take time to pray over each person who shares.

6. Read Acts 19:32. This is the mob mentality in action. People didn't even know what was going on, but they started shouting just because everyone else was shouting. What does this remind you of today? How do we navigate living in an instantaneous world that is easily offended? How do we make sure our responses are not merely reactions?

7. Acts 20:17-38 is perhaps one of the best displays of godly leadership in all of Scripture. Paul leads them by loving them. Reflect on the words Paul shares as well as the response of the elders at Ephesus. What does this teach us about real leadership? How is leading God's way different from how the world views leadership? What's one thing you see in this passage that is an area you need to work on personally?

Acts 21-23

COMMENTARY

21:1-3 This may simply seem like a recollection of their travels, but these details should also remind us this work was wearisome. Ministry is not promised to be easy, but we can be confident that it matters.

21:4-14 Paul is warned twice by other believers through the Holy Spirit that hardship awaits him in Jerusalem. Because Paul goes anyway, it naturally provides the question, *"Did Paul disobey the Holy Spirit?"* It's important to note the difference here. Agabus, in particular, prophesies that Paul will be arrested and imprisoned in Jerusalem. Upon hearing the prophecy, the disciples were the ones who urged Paul not to go. The Holy Spirit simply prepared Paul for what would happen to him in Jerusalem. How we interpret prophecy matters. God won't always provide prophecy so we can make efforts to change the future, but so we can be prepared for what will happen in the future.

21:5-6 It's subtle, but I couldn't help but notice that the disciples at Tyre who followed Paul and his companions to the ship so they could pray with him and say their goodbyes included entire families: husbands, wives, and children. And when Paul and his companions departed, the families returned home. Whether the result of busyness or just out of convenience, it's becoming rarer and rarer for families to do ministry or even take the time to fellowship with other believers together. I can think of all the "mom things" that had to have crossed the women's minds then too, such as *"It's dangerous by the water,"* or *"That's too far for the kids to walk."* But the desire to be with other disciples and to practice their faith as a family had more weight on how they made decisions. We have the same opportunities today. Let's prioritize them.

21:8-9 This is the same Philip mentioned earlier in the book of Acts. Cross-reference to Acts 6:5 and Acts 8:26-40.

21:9 Just a reminder that men and women are both recipients of the gift of prophecy. We don't use the word *"prophetess"* much anymore, but that title is how Philip's four daughters were known. And prayerfully, just as He did then, God will continue to raise up and use women through His gift of prophecy.

21:10-12 Agabus is the same prophet who foretold the famine in Jerusalem. *[To refresh your memory, refer to Acts 11:27-28.]* Because the disciples had already witnessed one of his prophecies fulfilled, that's likely the reason for their urgency in begging Paul not to go to Jerusalem.

21:13 Paul was moved by their love for him that desired to protect him, but he wanted to obey God more than he wanted to please them or he desired his own personal comfort. These words from Paul are a challenge and a reminder that the final say in how we should make decisions is our commitment to obey God.

21:17-20 Ministry is not a solo sport. We each have a role to play, but we are not alone in our calling. Find other disciples and spend time together. As Paul does here, celebrate what God is doing in your ministry, and praise Him together.

21:20-26 The mutual submission between James, Paul, and the elders of the Jerusalem church is really beautiful. Look out for others who are in ministry and learn from one another.

21:20-21 This is an example of how the truth can get twisted. Referring to the Jerusalem Council *(cross-reference to Acts 15)*, the Jews were falsely saying that Paul was teaching Jews to forsake Moses and traditional Jewish customs. All Paul said was that following Jewish customs were not required for salvation. He never said not to follow their traditional customs, but simply not to teach that the customs were required for salvation since salvation is only found through Christ.

21:23-26 Paul is not compromising his beliefs by purifying himself and taking a vow in the Jewish temple. He's merely trying to prove with his actions that the accusations against him are false. He doesn't believe following the Jewish customs are necessary for salvation, but he's also not trying to openly offend those who he wishes to reach with the gospel. This is a great example of what it looks like to be flexible on non-gospel issues for the sake of unity among believers. *[For more on this topic straight from Paul's heart, cross-reference to 1 Corinthians 9:19-23.]*

21:27-29 Paul faces another false accusation. Because Paul was seen in the city with Trophimus, from Ephesus, they assumed Paul also brought him into the temple with him. Since Trophimus was not Jewish, it would have been against the law for Paul to bring a Gentile into the temple.

21:30-36 Despite the best efforts of James and the Jerusalem church elders to protect Paul against false accusations, the mob mentality strikes again. Bringing a Gentile into the temple was a crime worthy of the death penalty, so Paul's enemies knew how to stir up the crowd to anger quickly. The confusion and emotion in the crowd quickly escalates to violence. It was only when the government officials showed up that Paul's beating stopped. By noting that Paul was bound by *"two chains,"* Luke is letting us know that Paul had a soldier on each side. As the tribune tried to learn what happened, *"he could not learn the facts because of the uproar."* Beware of reacting in situations that are filled with so much emotion that you cannot discern facts.

21:37-38 By Paul speaking Greek, he got the attention of the tribune. Possibly due to the harsh reaction of the crowd, the tribune assumed Paul was a different Jew who had caused trouble previously.

21:39- Despite being falsely accused and beaten, Paul still desired to speak to the people. But his goal wasn't to defend himself, but to share the gospel. Just as he had spoken in Greek to get the attention of the tribune, Paul speaks in Hebrew to get the attention of the Jews. Even though he has been mistreated, Paul is still looking for ways to show he respects their Jewish customs so they'll remain open to hearing the gospel.

22:3-5 Paul builds common ground with his accusers by extending grace to them, acknowledging they believed their motives were pure in arresting him. He also admits that in his life before Christ, he used to do the same thing to others that they are doing to him now.

22:6-21 After establishing common ground, Paul moves into sharing how his personal testimony reflects the message of the gospel. God has given each of us a story that points to His story. The gospel is not about us, but it is for us. When you share the gospel, make it personal. The gospel is not merely a matter of theology; it personally saves each one of us!

22:19-20 Like Paul, you may have parts of your past that aren't pretty. While we don't pride ourselves on our past sin, we also must realize that being honest about the grace God has shown us personally is a beautiful way for others to realize the depths of God's grace. Don't allow shame to prevent you from sharing the hard parts of your story when He prompts you to do so. God has redeemed every inch of your story for His use. His grace covers your shame.

22:22 The Jews were listening to Paul until he said the word, *"Gentiles."* It was like they believed him and his words about God until a certain line was crossed that merely offended their preferences and not their faith. My pastor, Bruce Frank, put it this way one time, and I've never forgotten it: *"Be careful with your preferences so that they don't become your prejudices."*

22:23-24 Paul's association with the Gentiles is what started the crowd's violence in the first place. And even after hearing the gospel and Paul's testimony, the crowd's hard hearts caused them to resort to violence again. To examine Paul by flogging is not a light punishment, but severe torture. Often, flogging was a beating so severe that many who were flogged did not live through it.

22:25-29 It's unlikely that Paul suddenly remembered it's against the law to bind a Roman citizen without a fair trial. But Paul was first concerned with defending the gospel, and then, he was concerned with defending himself. Self-preservation is a natural human response, which is why we must be intentional to walk in the Spirit and not merely exist in the flesh. Roman citizenship was something that could be purchased, which is what the tribune had done, but Paul was a Roman citizen by birth. Being born Roman was considered higher than paid citizenship, which is why Paul's punishment was not carried out. Be careful not to miss the big picture of our intentional God and His protection. Even the city where Paul was born was not an accident but was part of God's plan for Paul from the beginning.

22:30 Paul was not harmed further, but he also was not released. And although the high priest was in violation of the law himself by having Paul struck, Paul was also wrong for speaking evil of a ruler of the people. Again, rather than defending his actions or claiming that they are both guilty, Paul both acknowledges his error and again tries to build common ground with the Jews by quoting the Old Testament law.

23:5 Cross-reference to Exodus 22:28.

23:6-10 This might be one of my favorite side stories from Paul's ministry. Realizing that there were both Pharisees and Sadducees present and knowing that these groups disagree on the resurrection, Paul took the attention off of himself by making an issue between them instead. Paul was also speaking truth when he said with respect to *"the hope and resurrection of the dead that I am on trial."* The gospel all hinges on the hope we have because of Jesus' death and resurrection.

23:11 Not only does Jesus comfort Paul, but Paul gets a glimpse of a future assignment: he will testify in Rome just as he has done in Jerusalem.

23:12-15 In their anger, the Jews were able to convince themselves they were doing God's work by conspiring to kill Paul even though murder violates one of the Ten Commandments. The things God calls you to do will never contradict Scripture.

23:16 This is one of the only mentions that we have of Paul's family in Scripture. God put Paul's nephew in the right place at the right time to hear of the conspiracy so he could warn Paul.

23:17-22 Again, it was likely the perks of being a Roman citizen that allowed Paul to have visitors in prison while he awaited his trial, as well as privileged favor among the centurions and the tribune.

23:22 We don't know the exact age of Paul's nephew, but we gather he was young since Luke describes him as the *"son of Paul's sister."* He may have been young, but he was able to be used by God to spare Paul from senseless murder. Scripture is full of these examples, so we must never forget that age has no bearing on your usability to God.

23:23-25 At this time, there would have been a total of around 1,000 Roman soldiers in Jerusalem. If you want an accurate picture of how seriously Roman citizens were protected, do the math of these numbers, and you can see they deployed nearly half of their soldiers in the city to protect Paul.

23:26-30 Claudius does a good job of elevating himself over actual events in his letter to Felix. He didn't exactly "rescue" Paul. He was about to have him flogged until Paul volunteered the knowledge that he was a Roman citizen. But also, there's a lot to learn from how Luke records these events. Rather than directly calling out Claudius' character and false recollection of Paul's arrest and treatment in Jerusalem, he simply shares what the letter said and lets the facts speak for themselves. It's possible to simply share the story without crossing over into slander.

23:31-35 Every time Paul is moved, he is given the opportunity to share the gospel in a higher court in front of higher ranking officials. Though it's much easier for us to zoom out and see the big picture of that opportunity now, I'm sure, in real time, it felt tiresome and even tedious at times to Paul, his travel companions, and even the other believers. It's important that even when we are in the thick of it that we trust God, knowing His plan will always work out for His glory and for good.

Acts 21-23

QUESTIONS

Icebreaker: Paul gets an opportunity to share his testimony in front of a group of angry Jews, and they were willing to listen to him until he said the word, *"Gentiles."* On a much lighter note, what's one word someone could say to you that would bring you to a hard stop? *(I'll go first: I'd like you to meet my pet bird...." I'm out at bird. Not a fan.)*

1. It would be an easy detail to glance over, but in Acts 21:5-6, we see that the whole family *(husbands, wives, and children)* followed Paul to his ship when he left Tyre. It's certainly easier to "divide and conquer" in terms of trying to do ministry and have gospel-centered conversations with young kids in tow. But in terms of discipling our kids, are we supposed to pursue ease? What are some simple ways you can integrate family discipleship into your home, just like these families who traveled as a family for Paul's departure?

2. Read Acts 21:4 and Acts 21:11 aloud. Because Paul chooses to go to Jerusalem anyway, it almost appears like Paul may disobey the Holy Spirit. Do you think Paul disobeys the Holy Spirit, or was the prophecy preparation for Paul for what would happen in Jerusalem instead of prevention?

3. Read aloud Paul's reply in Acts 21:13 to the disciples who were urging him to go to Jerusalem. We see Paul's compassion for people and his conviction of God's mission. What do his words remind us should get the final say when we are making important decisions?

4. Acts 21:17-26 shows the connection between Paul, James, and the elders of the Jerusalem church. They are celebrating what God is doing, listening to one another, looking out for each other, and putting mutual submission into practice. We see examples of Paul not following the advice of the believers in Tyre who do not want him to go to Jerusalem and we also see him following the wisdom given to him when he arrives in Jerusalem. These back-to-back

interactions demonstrate the importance of loving God and others, but pleasing God alone. We're not called to people-pleasing, but we're also not called to isolation. Most people struggle with one or the other. Which one is harder for you: the desire to please people or the temptation to isolate yourself from others?

5. Paul does not compromise his beliefs by purifying himself and taking a vow in the Jewish temple when he arrives in Jerusalem. He doesn't believe following the Jewish customs are necessary for salvation, but he's also not trying to openly offend those who he wishes to reach with the gospel. This is a great example of what it looks like to be flexible on non-gospel issues for the sake of unity among believers. What are some examples of how we can handle non-gospel issues in a flexible way for the sake of unity?

6. Paul is able to extend grace to the angry Jewish mob largely because he has experienced God's grace for himself. The two usually work together. If you struggle to extend grace to others, you probably struggle to give grace to yourself too. Have you found this to be true in your life? How do we move forward in accepting God's grace for ourselves so we can extend God's grace to others?

7. Every time Paul is moved, he is given the opportunity to share the gospel in a higher court in front of higher ranking officials. Though it's much easier for us to zoom out and see the big picture of that opportunity now, I'm sure, in real time, it felt tiresome and even tedious, at times to Paul, his travel companions and even the other believers. It's important that even when we are in the thick of it that we ask God to trust Him and His plan, knowing it will always work out for His glory and for good. What's a way you stay encouraged to keep an eternal perspective when you're in a weary season?

Acts 24-26

COMMENTARY

24:1 At the end of the last chapter, Paul was put in prison and told his trial would begin when his accusers arrived. Five days later, Paul's trial begins. Keep in mind that this means Paul's accusers traveled 60 miles on foot to falsely accuse him. Sometimes, people will go to great lengths to oppose Kingdom efforts. But despite what it may seem is happening through people, remember that your battle is not against people but against one enemy. Cross-reference to Ephesians 6:12 for more from Paul on this.

24:2-4 Tertullus' opening arguments in court are full of lies. His first lies centered in flattery for Felix. He called him *"most excellent Felix"* and claimed *"everywhere"* and in *"every way"* to be full of gratitude for him, even though Felix was widely hated by the Jews. He claimed they enjoyed *"much peace"* and the *"reforms being made for the nation"* when truthfully, Felix had more conflict during his reign than any other Roman government before him. He stroked Felix's ego by claiming to not want to tie up his time because of his importance and for him to hear them *"briefly in his kindness"* knowing full well that Felix was more known for his dishonesty than his kindness. Beware of flattery. Just because words sound good, that doesn't mean they're true. Weigh flowery words against facts when you're struggling to be swayed by mere words that sound good.

24:5-8 Tertullus continues with his lies, but this time, he moves from flattering Felix to falsely accusing Paul. Paul always entered into Jewish temples to reason from the Scriptures, and riots were always initiated by the crowds, not by Paul or any of the apostles. He used divisive language like "sect" and "ringleader" to describe Paul. And he claimed Paul profaned the temple and they "seized him," implying both his own heroism as well as implying that Paul was caught with a Gentile in the temple, when in reality, he was merely seen speaking to a Gentile outside of the temple. His accusations add up to three different charges against Paul: stirring up riots, being a ringleader of Christians, and profaning the Jewish temple.

24:9-10 It's a simple sentence, but vs. 9 is a picture of what it must have felt like in that room to be Paul; it would have been easy to look around and give up because everyone around you is against you. But his cheerful *(by his own words!)* defense can only be explained by the fact that while Paul may have been the only one to defend himself in the courtroom, Paul was not alone. God was with him. And God's side, even if it's just God and you against a room full of many others, is always the majority.

24:11-13 In total contrast to Tertullus' words that are emotional, persuasive, and flattering, Paul sticks to the facts. He dismisses the first charge quickly about starting riots, saying he did not dispute anyone or stir up any crowd in the temple or the city, and that they have zero evidence to prove that he did.

24:14-16 Instead of continuing to defend himself, Paul confesses to the second charge, that he was a leader of Christianity. What he does, though, is challenge their view of Christianity. Though they claim it to be a "sect," Paul proves that Christianity doesn't dismiss the Law and the Prophets. Rather than dividing from his accusers, Paul seeks unity by agreeing with them that his hope is in the same God and that there will be a final judgment. In the moments when you need discernment in a disagreement, you can usually get some clarity by paying attention to who pursues unity and who pursues division. Andy Stanley said it best: "Disagreement is avoidable. But division is always a choice."

24:18-19 Here, Paul begins to confront the third charge when he realizes the Jews from Asia were actually the real ones who were accusing Paul of causing trouble, and they are not even there. According to Roman law, your accuser must confront you face-to-face. So while Paul has replied to their accusation, he also makes it clear that the men accusing him are the ones who saw him enter the temple to be purified, not the ones who saw him begin any riots.

24:20-21 Paul refers back to what happened before the council in Acts 23, again claiming to be on trial with respect to resurrection from the dead. Again, more than believing in the resurrection, Paul is redirecting the conversation back to an opportunity that will allow him to share the gospel. He does not want to argue about resurrection generally, but he wants to specifically share about Jesus' resurrection. In disagreements, aim to get back to the gospel as quickly as you possibly can.

24:22-23 Felix may have had an accurate view of Christianity because his wife was Jewish. Either way, he ends the accusations against Paul and decides he will deal with his case at a later time. The freedoms Paul is given, though a prisoner on trial, is again, largely because he is a Roman citizen.

24:24-26 At first, it can seem encouraging that Felix is bringing his wife to have conversations with Paul and allows Paul the opportunity to share with them about Jesus. But Felix's motives are not pure. He's not eager to learn about Jesus. He's hoping that Paul will bribe him with money for his release. So for that reason alone, because it would have been against the law for a prisoner to bribe a leader to allow him to be released, he continuously positions Paul to be around him, hoping that a bribe offer will come. People who compromise their character will probably put you in positions to compromise yours. But Paul never resorts to bribery to break out of prison. And he didn't back down from the truth either, even resulting with Felix being *"alarmed"* by Paul's blunt commitment to the full gospel.

24:27 This is one of those moments where I wish we could hang in the tension here and slow down to let it sink in that these conversations between Paul and Felix didn't happen merely over days or weeks, but for *two. whole. years.* I can only imagine how easy it would have been for Paul to be frustrated because it appears Felix knows Paul is innocent, but rather than do the right thing, Felix is more concerned with appeasing the Jews. But easy or not, waiting is part of the Christian life. We move on God's time, not ours. And waiting is never wasted when we wait with God. We may not know the exact specifics of what Paul did over these two years, but we know that while in prison in general, he wrote many of the letters that made it in the New Testament. He frequently shared the gospel with both jailers and fellow prisoners. He didn't focus on what he couldn't do for the Kingdom because he was waiting, but he did what he could for the Kingdom while he was waiting. May that be a lesson for us too.

25:1-5 There is a lot of talk about doing *"favors"* in these verses that merits a definition reminder. A "favor" would be an unmerited act of kindness done purely out of goodwill. But what the Jews and the leaders are calling "favors" is actually *favoritism* – to be treated with partiality over another. It's important to notice the difference. And while it may look like Festus protected Paul, he had no idea of the plans of the ambush and likely was just wanting to make sure he received credit for whatever he decided to do with Paul. God is the one who protected Paul against the plot to kill him.

25:7-9 Notice that the charges they brought against Paul were *"many"* and *"serious"* though they could not be proven. Paul articulates clearly he had not broken Jewish law, the temple laws, or Roman law. And though Festus offers to have the trial in his court, Festus' motives are also revealed: he does want to gain favor with the Jews. Felix appeased the Jews by keeping Paul in prison, but Festus knows he can win favor with the Jews by convicting Paul and having him killed.

25:10-12 This reply from Paul not only shows his intelligence, but his courage. Paul, well-educated in Roman law, knows that as a Roman citizen, he has the right to be tried by Caesar in Caesar's court. And while appealing to Caesar will take him to Rome *(which has been his ministry goal for quite some time at this point)*, it also raises the stakes for his punishment if he is convicted. But caring about the opportunity for the gospel more than he cared about his own life and safety, Paul shows he believed it would be better to go to Rome as a prisoner than not be able to get to Rome at all.

25:13-22 Paul has appealed to Caesar, so that is the next trial that will count. But when King Agrippa comes to town, Festus uses Paul's imprisonment as an attempt to impress him. And although this "mock trial" of sorts results from impure motives, it still gives Paul another opportunity to present the gospel. For Paul, being on trial was never about the opportunity to present his case, but about being able to present the gospel. When you encounter "extra steps" as you go about your life, see them as extra opportunities to plant seeds about Christ instead of merely inconveniences.

25:19 Festus didn't know much about Christianity, but he understood enough to know that the resurrection was central. Paul had shared the gospel with enough boldness, that even though Festus didn't know much, he knew the main thing. Our goals should be similar in communicating with those who do not know much about Jesus.

25:23 Picture it. Hear the trumpets and the drums. See the royal robes and the fine jewelry. Imagine the crowds gathering trying to get a glimpse of the king, amidst tons of soldiers and all of the most important people of the city, all trying to look more important than they actually are… and then, Paul is brought in. It had to have been quite the show, especially after Paul had spent two years in prison.

25:24-27 The flattery is back, and Festus' flattery of King Agrippa might actually be more sugary sweet than the Jews' fake flattery to Felix. *(Note "especially before you, King Agrippa" in verse 26!)* And while this is intended to be nothing more than to satisfy Festus' desire for approval from both the Jews and King Agrippa, God uses it for so much more.

26:1-3 Paul began by 1) reminding King Agrippa that he is familiar with both the *"customs and controversies"* of the Jews. Paul gently leads him to see this unbiased, though Festus and the crowd are leaning toward his guilt. 2) He also asked King Agrippa to listen to him patiently. He sets up that he's going to tell the whole story, which allows him the opportunity to give the most detailed account and full expression of the gospel yet. And though counter-intuitive to human logic, the higher the official before Paul, the bolder he was.

26:4-7 Again, Paul begins with facts. He talks about his early life, which all of the Jews know. But beyond the facts of his early life, Paul establishes facts of the Jewish faith to recognize that if he's on trial for what he believes, then really, all Jews should be on trial.

26:8 Once again appealing to their faith, Paul clearly establishes that because of the belief they have in God, they, too, should recognize that the resurrection was possible for God.

26:9-11 Before Paul accuses them of opposing him because of Jesus, Paul owns how he used to oppose those who followed Jesus too. In a normal "trial" setting, this would have not been a great way to build his case by claiming he's also done what his accusers are doing. This is more proof that Paul was interested in presenting the gospel, not his case.

26:14 *"It's hard for you to kick against the goads"* was a cultural expression everyone in the courtroom would have been familiar with. Today, we understand it better as: "It's hard for you to go against the will of God."

26:16 Note the two roles Paul recalls being given by Jesus: 1) **servant** and 2) **witness**. Not preacher. Not leader. Not writer. But servant and witness. For all who have accepted His free gift of salvation and follow Him, those are our top two roles too.

26:18 Paul is clear about the transformation that occurs when we share the gospel and it's accepted by someone else: 1) their eyes are opened, 2) they turn from darkness to light, 3) they turn from the power of Satan to God, 3) they receive forgiveness of sins, 4) they receive a place among those who are sanctified by faith in Jesus. So many times, we allow fear of rejection to prevent us from sharing the gospel. We need to constantly remind ourselves of what we are risking others missing out on when we refuse to share the gospel because of the possibility of rejection. Remember that it's not your job to convince someone to follow Christ. It's just your job to share what He has done for them.

26:19 Paul is showing respect to King Agrippa, but he's also making it clear that he obeys God.

26:20 A reminder: repentance is a change in direction. So we repent and turn toward God, and then we *"perform deeds in keeping with their repentance."* Good works do not save us, but they show we are turned toward the Lord. I love the way Martin Luther put it: "God doesn't need our good works; our neighbor does." Good works follow genuine heart change. We should act in such a way that reflects our repentance.

26:20-23 Again, Paul clearly shares the gospel, showing that Jesus was the Savior promised by all the Old Testament prophets, and that the gospel was for everyone, both the Jews and the Gentiles.

26:22 Paul has spent two years in prison, but he acknowledges that he has never been alone. God has been with him and been his help.

26:24-25 Knowing Festus' motives, it's as if he has been waiting on a break in Paul's words with this planned response, no matter what Paul said. There was nothing outlandish or outrageous about what Paul said. Paul again shows respect for Festus but sticks to the facts.

26:26-27 Paul replies to Festus, but turns his attention back to King Agrippa. He knows that Agrippa is familiar with Jewish beliefs, so again, Paul is not concerned with building his case. He just wants to make sure King Agrippa fully understands the gospel.

26:28 Agrippa responds to Paul's genuine care with sarcasm. Again, no one is too far gone for God to reach. But remember the pomp and fanfare for King Agrippa's arrival. By the world's standards, Agrippa has it all: fame, power, money, servants, etc. The more that this world has its grip on you, the harder it will be for you to let go and grab hold of God. Beware of how much you allow yourselves to be caught up in the things of this world. It may prevent you from realizing your need for God.

26:29 No question about it, Paul's deepest desire was for others to accept Christ's free gift of salvation. So even when he's taunted with sarcasm, he replies genuinely.

26:30-32 If Paul had chosen not to appeal to Caesar and had agreed to be tried in Festus' court, at this point, he would have been free to go. But Paul had already made his decision. His ultimate goal was not his own freedom, but to share the gospel in Rome. It will be quite the adventure to get there, but his destination is finally set: Paul is headed to Rome to appeal before Caesar.

Acts 24-26

QUESTIONS

Icebreaker: When beginning his defense in front of King Agrippa, Paul says, "I consider myself fortunate to stand before you today." After being in prison for two whole years, Paul still feels fortunate. What a beautiful reminder that our attitude is everything! Being completely honest with yourself: do you usually have a cup half-empty or half-full perspective? What steps can you take today to remain grateful despite your circumstances?

1. Read Acts 24:2-4 aloud. Do you hear the flattery in Tertullus' words? He paints a picture of a peaceful reign and relationship between Felix and the Jews, but truthfully, Felix was a dishonest leader who had more conflict in his reign than any other leader before him. Why would Tertullus lie about reality? What's the difference between flattery and admiration? How can we tell the difference so we cannot be deceived by words that sound good but are not true?

2. Acts 24:9 tells us the crowd joined in the charge, affirming the false accusations against Paul. But despite being wildly outnumbered, Paul replies that he will *"cheerfully"* make his defense. If you were the only one to defend yourself in a courtroom full of opposition, do you think you would be making your defense *cheerfully?* What do you think gave Paul this perspective?

3. Both times Paul gives his defense, he confirms everything he believes that the Jews also believe. Though he is being falsely accused, rather than argue his innocence, Paul is still trying to pursue unity and to share the gospel. Andy Stanley put it this way: "Disagreement is avoidable. But division is always a choice." How have you personally chosen unity when given the opportunity to choose division in a disagreement? What was the fruit of that?

4. Paul is in prison under Felix for two years. We know now that time was not wasted because during that time, Paul wrote many of the letters that made it in the New Testament, and he frequently shared the gospel with both jailers and fellow prisoners. Have you experienced a season of waiting? How did God use you during that time, and what did you learn during your season of waiting?

5. By appealing to Caesar, Paul increased his chance of greater punishment, but he believed that it would be better to go to Rome as a prisoner than not be able to get to Rome at all. Paul demonstrated over and over again that he cared more about the opportunity to spread the gospel than he cared about his own life and safety. What can we learn from his example when we encounter "extra steps" as we go about our own lives? How can we see these as extra opportunities to plant seeds for Christ rather than as inconveniences? Read Acts 26:18 for Paul's reminder of what happens when someone believes the gospel. If we allow our fear of rejection to prevent us from sharing the gospel with someone, we miss out on sharing the opportunity for: 1) their eyes to be opened, 2) a turn from darkness to light, 3) a turn from the power of Satan to God, 3) their forgiveness of sins, 4) their place among those who are sanctified by faith in Jesus. It's not your job to convince someone to follow Christ. It's just your job to share what He has done for them. Who do you know that you are praying will accept Christ? Pray for everyone mentioned by name as you close your group in prayer.

6. Read Acts 26:20 aloud. Paul says he has encouraged everyone to repent, turn toward God, and to perform deeds in keeping with their repentance. What do you think that last phrase means: *"to perform deeds in keeping with their repentance"*? What are some of the most helpful spiritual habits/rhythms you put into practice to help align your actions with your beliefs?

Acts 27-28

COMMENTARY

27:1-3 Though you would assume the relationship between prison guard and prisoner would be one of conflict, Paul and Julius seem to have mutual respect for one another built on trust. Some say that Paul was given extra freedoms because he was a Roman citizen, but Luke intentionally says that *"Julius treated Paul kindly."* Even though Paul's a prisoner, Julius allows him to go to his "friends" to be cared for, which we know are the believers that are in the port city, so Paul is continuing to minister as he travels.

27:4-12 The details provided here should ultimately point us to God's protection of Paul so he could get to Rome and share the gospel there. Multiple times, the ship is pushed off course by opposing winds. By giving us an idea of the timeline surrounding the Fast, which took place in the fall around The Day of Atonement, we know the Mediterranean Sea was largely considered "untravelable" around mid-November through the winter months. Paul, an experienced sailor, knew this and warned the captain of the likely danger ahead. But the captain of the ship dismissed the warning from Paul and decided to try to make it to the port at Crete so they could be at a larger port for the winter months and continue their voyage in the Spring. Even though Paul ended up being right in his assessment of the potential danger, he doesn't grow angry or frustrated when his advice is ignored. He continues to use his time to witness to those with him on the ship.

27:13-20 Unless you have experience with sailing, it's hard to follow along with what's happening in these verses. But basically, everything that *could* go wrong *does* go wrong. They are in the middle of one of the most unpredictable storms. Just when they move past one disaster, they encounter another. Imagine the worst storm you've ever experienced, but take away the comfort of watching it from indoors. Put yourself in the middle of extreme darkness, howling winds and waves infinitely larger than your ship. And even when the chaos stops, the stillness isn't comforting either, because it reminds you of how large the ocean is and that you have no way of knowing where you are or how to get back to shore. This is before the invention of the compass, so with no sight of land and no sun or stars to provide any direction, those on board are utterly hopeless as to how they could possibly make it back to land safely.

27:21-22 Paul did predict their trip would go exactly as it did. He mentions this, not to rub it in their faces that he was right and they were wrong, but he's working to establish trust so they'll listen to what he has to say about God.

27:23 I love the phrase Paul uses to describe his relationship with the Lord: *"to whom I belong and whom I worship."* We respond to belonging to God by worshiping Him. Also note that before Paul shares what God said to him, he clearly identifies who God is to him. But also a note for each of us: the more aware you are of who God is, the more clarity with which you will hear Him speak. It's hard to hear His voice if you're unclear of who He is.

27:24-26 The men and Paul had every right to be fearful of what was to come. But when it doesn't look like there is any chance of their survival, Paul gives them hope by reminding them that God is still with them. Because of the angel's words to him, Paul is sure he will stand before Caesar, which means they will all arrive safely in Rome. That doesn't change the fact, though, that their surrounding circumstances all indicate a safe arrival is nearly impossible. Paul is acting on faith in God, not confidence in his circumstances. We will all encounter similar situations in life. Head knowledge of the Lord is good, but head knowledge will not be of any benefit if it doesn't transfer into faith that you put into practice. Let your faith in God, who He is and what He can do, determine your confidence, not your circumstances.

27:27-32 Larger boats have smaller boats on board for emergencies. The sailors had essentially decided to save themselves. They were going to get the one remaining small boat and get safely to shore themselves. Doing so would have left no one behind with the knowledge of how to steer the larger ship back to safety. So because of Paul's wisdom in speaking up, the soldiers were able to cut the lines of the smaller boat so the sailors would have no choice but to remain on board and do their best to not just save their own lives, but to get everyone on board to safety. This decision continued to build Paul's rapport with the centurion, soldiers, and guards. They did not listen to him the first time he spoke up, but they followed his advice this time.

27:33-34 The storm has been so rough that they have not been able to prepare food for two weeks. Paul knows they will hit land soon, so they all need to be strong enough to do whatever they will need to do to survive. Paul also reminds them again of the hope God has given them.

27:35-37 Paul praised God for delivering them before God actually delivered them. Paul's confidence in God was so great that he could actually praise God for the outcome before it even happened, and his confidence in God encouraged all 276 people on board.

27:38 The lighter the ship was, the more that would help when they reached land. And while that seemed logical, this still took a tremendous amount of faith to get rid of their remaining food sources.

27:39-41 Today, this beach is known as St. Paul's Bay. The ship struck into a reef, making the bow *(the forward part of the ship)* stick into the land, while the pounding surf broke up the stern *(the back of the ship)*. The ship is literally torn into pieces.

27:42 Since the soldiers were responsible for their prisoners with their own lives, the soldiers made the decision to kill their prisoners to save themselves because they figured if they didn't kill them, the prisoners would escape.

27:43 The centurion wishes to save Paul, so all the prisoners end up being spared. But why does he want to save Paul? The most logical explanation is because Paul made efforts to save him when the sailors were plotting to save themselves. But we also cannot forget God's promise to spare Paul so he could testify before Caesar. More than crediting the centurion for wanting to

27:44 The image of all 276 people coming safely to land, in addition to the fact that none of the prisoners tried to run, leaves me the same kind of dumbfounded as I was when none of the prisoners tried to escape in Acts 16. At two different times, why would prisoners not take their chance to escape? The only explanation is that they felt like they were part of something bigger than their own personal freedom. Paul gave them glimpses of God, and they desired to be part of it.

28:1-6 God allowed the shipwreck, but spared Paul's life. He also allowed the snake to bite Paul, but protected him from harm. God's protection does not always fully prevent us from danger, which goes beyond our human logic and understanding. You will have to activate your faith in the moments when God's protection does not prevent danger.

28:1 Malta is a small island, at only about 18 miles long and 8 miles wide. Not only would it have been difficult to land on such a small island, but they are also miraculously still en route to Rome. These facts are further evidence that God was with them.

28:2 In case your Bible translation refers to the natives as *"barbarians,"* that term merely meant they were islanders who did not speak Greek. They were not savages, as is widely associated with that term today. Still, though, the natives' kindness in building them a fire to welcome them would have been unusual, just for the fact that this was a small island. It would have been easy for them to assume 276 people landing all at once was an attack, but these islanders chose to welcome them with kindness.

28:3-4 Can you imagine surviving a shipwreck only to be bitten by a deadly snake? The natives reveal their religious beliefs when this happens to Paul, saying that since Justice *(a Greek goddess also known as Dike or Dice)* hadn't been able to kill him at sea, she would get her revenge on Paul through the snake. Similar to the "karma" belief that is widespread today that what goes around comes around, the natives say Paul must be guilty of murder for Justice to repay him like this.

28:5-6 Their beliefs quickly changed about Paul, when they saw that he merely shook the snake off. No swelling. No sickness. They now believe Paul to be a god, which Paul knew would open their hearts to listen to him when he shared about who he knew to be God.

28:7-10 Read these verses again, remembering that Paul is a shipwrecked, snake-bitten prisoner. Despite great hardship, Paul never lost sight of the mission. He could have claimed he needed rest after such a hard journey. But instead, he ministered greatly to the people of Malta. Serving the Lord is different from work we do in our own strength. God supplies all we need to do what He calls us to do. Paul is not superhuman. He simply ministered to them while relying on God as his Power Source instead of merely relying on his own strength.

28:11-13 It's easy to gloss over these verses, as they merely dictate the route of their travels. But try to slow yourself down and recognize how much time is passing by. It would have been easy for Paul to grow impatient or to lose passion for sharing the gospel in Rome when so much time had passed. But despite delays and setbacks, Paul remains confident in his call to share the gospel in Rome.

28:14 The *"brothers"* here are believers, so the gospel has reached Rome before Paul got there. Though Paul was likely accompanied by a guard, he was still allowed the freedom to stay with Christians at Puteoli for a full week.

28:15a Believers came from as far as 40 miles away to meet Paul and his travel companions. Though that may not seem like a great distance today, remember that these believers would have traveled on foot for several days to be here to meet Paul. Paul wrote the Letter to the Romans while he was living in Corinth *(recorded in Acts 18)*. Though this is Paul's first trip to Rome, Paul already knew many of the believers in Rome. [To see this clearly, turn in your Bible to Romans 16. In this chapter alone, Paul mentions 29 people by name.]

28:15b Note the two things seeing the believers prompted Paul to do: *thank God* and *take courage*. We should view one another in similar ways. 1) The way we minister to one another should ultimately remind us that God put us in one another's lives.

Remember that the people God puts in your life are gifts from Him. 2) The people of Rome couldn't really do anything to help Paul. He is still a prisoner, and he will have to give his own defense before Caesar. But there is something very real about the ministry of presence. Ministering to one another won't always mean you have the answer someone needs or be the solution to their problem. But your presence alone could put courage in them. Don't let the fact that you can't "do anything" stop you from showing up. Sometimes, just being there for someone is all you need to do to minister to them.

28:16 Paul is still a prisoner, but rather than being confined to a public jail, his imprisonment is more comparable to house arrest.

28:17 As a prisoner under house arrest, Paul was unable to travel to the synagogues. But he could ask the local Jewish leaders to come to him, so that's exactly what he did.

28:18-19 The Jews repeatedly falsely accused Paul. Though he would have been justified in doing so, Paul chose not to accuse his accusers of wrongdoing. Why? Because more than making an enemy out of anyone, Paul desired for his Jewish brothers to meet Jesus the way he had. A reminder for us: just because you are justified to accuse someone, that doesn't always mean you should. Before you accuse, think about how your accusation will hinder or propel the gospel. Let the speed of the gospel help you discern your decision.

28:20 *"The hope of Israel"* Paul speaks of is Jesus.

28:21-22 It's highly unlikely that the Jews are being honest with Paul. It's difficult to believe that they could be familiar with the great opposition of Christianity and be unfamiliar with Paul. And while the words *"this sect"* when translated into English sound really innocent, the root word of the word used in the Greek *[tēs haireseōs]* is the same word that we derive the term *"heresy"* from. So while they are probably honest about their curiosity to hear straight from Paul, they are also more concerned with ensuring neither the Jewish leaders in Jerusalem nor the governing officials of Rome associate them as agreeing with Paul.

28:23 The second group of Jewish leaders who came to visit Paul was bigger than the first group. And while we don't have a recording of what was said in those meetings, it's likely that Paul spoke to the Jews 1) about what they already believed about God and 2) how Jesus was part of God's plan from the beginning. Luke uses words to describe Paul's words like *"expounded," "testifying,"* and *"trying to convince them."* It's more important that we note he never tried to persuade them outside of the gospel. Persuasion is not bad in itself, but it's easy to get misplaced when we attempt to persuade outside of the gospel.

28:24-25 This is not the first time this text has been quoted in the New Testament. Jesus also referred back to the words of Isaiah in Matthew 13:14-15 and John 12:39-40. Basically, Isaiah was predicting that some would reject the gospel, not because it wasn't true, but because of the hardness of their own hearts. No doubt, this was a hard message to receive, which is why it causes a mixed response from the Jews.

28:26-27 Cross-reference to Isaiah 6:9-10.

28:28 *"They will listen"* may be the three most powerful words we still need to heed today. What God has done is done, and His plan will prevail. But what makes the difference for each of us is whether or not we choose to listen.

28:29 You may be reading from a translation that skips from verse 28 to verse 30 or your translation may include verse 29, but it has brackets around it. Basically, Biblical scholars are unsure about this verse: whether it was written by Luke or if it was added to Acts by a later scribe. Depending on the translation you have, they either made the choice to omit it completely, or to set it apart with brackets to indicate that it's unknown whether or not those words were part of Luke's original manuscript.

28:30-31 When Paul first began to dream about the day when he would minister and share the gospel in Rome, I doubt he pictured it the way it ended up: arriving in Rome as a prisoner under house arrest. But instead of focusing on his restrictions, Luke records that Paul ministered *"with all boldness and without hindrance."* Worldly limitations will not necessarily hold you back from the ministry God has called you to do. Focus on what you can do, and trust God for the rest.

Acts 27-28

QUESTIONS

Icebreaker: From the beginning, Paul (the prisoner) and Julias (the prison guard) treat one another with mutual respect, which tends to dismantle the potential for conflict, proving that just because there's *typically* tension in that relationship, it doesn't *have* to be that way. Do you have a relationship in your life that is uncommonly positive, such as one with a business rival or an in-law? What do you attribute to being the main reason your relationship is an exception to the typical clash?

1. Acts 27:35 records that Paul thanked God before the ship came ashore. He was confident that what God told him was true, so he worshiped God before He rescued them. Have you ever praised and worshiped God before an outcome? How do you think worshiping God affects your confidence in Him?

2. None of the prisoners took their chance to escape in the midst of the shipwreck. Why wouldn't they run? How do you think we can live in such a way that shows others glimpses of God more than they just see us?

3. God didn't provide a smooth landing for the ship or prevent the snake from biting Paul. God's protection for Paul included both a shipwreck and a snake bite. What He did was spare Paul's life in the shipwreck and allowed Paul to suffer no harm from the bite. How can we adjust our perspective to see God's protection when we're still in a situation we deem dangerous?

4. Paul may have been a shipwrecked, snake-bitten prisoner, but he still ministered greatly to the people of Malta. Transparently, many have probably quit serving over much less severe circumstances. Despite what the people of Malta thought, Paul was not a god himself, but he did rely on God's power more than his own strength. When you feel like you've exhausted your own strength and reached the limit of what you can do, how do you let God take over and continue to minister through you?

5. Read Acts 28:15 aloud. What does the text say seeing the believers who came to greet Paul prompt him to do? What do these two things remind us about how we should view our relationships with one another?

6. When Paul first began to dream about the day when he would minister and share the gospel in Rome, I doubt he pictured it the way it ended up: arriving in Rome as a prisoner under house arrest. But instead of focusing on his restrictions, Luke records that Paul ministered *"with all boldness and without hindrance."* Worldly limitations will not necessarily hold you back from the ministry God has called you to do. What do you think is a limitation you believe holds you back from the ministry God has called you to do? What's one step you can take that focuses more on what you can do instead of choosing to focus on what's holding you back?

7. Acts seems to end abruptly without any resolution as to what happened to Paul, especially when he was finally able to stand before Caesar in Rome. But truthfully, the reason why it doesn't really "end" is because the gospel movement recorded in Acts is the same gospel movement we are still part of today. The story of the church is still being written. Read Acts 28:30 together as our marching orders for how we continue the gospel movement in our world today. What do you think it looks like practically to *"Proclaim the Kingdom of God and teach about the Lord Jesus Christ with all boldness and without hindrance?"* How has studying the book of Acts inspired you to continue the gospel movement in your life today?

Three

CONCLUDING THOUGHTS

---

1. The book of Acts ends abruptly because the story of the gospel movement is still being written today.

> Acts is the earliest record of church history. It seems to end abruptly without any resolution as to what happened to Paul, especially when he was finally able to stand before Caesar in Rome. But truthfully, the reason why it doesn't really "end" is because the gospel movement recorded in Acts is the same gospel movement we are still part of today. The story of the church is still being written. Let's take Acts 28:30 as our marching orders for how we continue to take the gospel forward: *"proclaiming the Kingdom of God and teaching about the Lord Jesus Christ with all boldness and without hindrance."*

2. God was in full control of Paul's time in prison.

> In addition to the people Paul was able to welcome into his home to share the gospel during his time in house arrest, Paul also used the break in his travel to write letters to the churches, which we know today as several of the Epistles of the New Testament. During this house arrest, most Biblical scholars agree this was when Paul wrote Ephesians, Philippians, Colossians, and Philemon. So while it could have seemed that his circumstances limited Paul's ministry, the fact that his letters were included in the New Testament, this imprisonment actually expanded the ministry Paul was able to do far past the span of merely his own lifetime.

3. What happened during the rest of Paul's ministry?

It seems super anticlimactic to see such a build-up of Paul getting to Rome, and other than us hearing that Paul shared the gospel under house arrest for two years, Luke doesn't record what happened when Paul stood before Caesar. While the Bible doesn't record it, there are extra biblical historical resources that tell us what happened to Paul. According to these historical texts, Paul was eventually released from this imprisonment. Upon his release, he took the gospel further west, possibly as far as Spain. Later, Paul returns to Rome as a prisoner again. But this time, instead of being released, he was martyred. To our best guess, Paul's 2nd letter to Timothy was written during his second imprisonment in Rome while he awaited execution.

Recommended Resources

FOR DEEPER STUDY

Strong's Exhaustive Concordance of the Bible
Strong, James. *The New Strong's Exhaustive Concordance of the Bible : With Main Concordance, Appendix to the Main Concordance, Hebrew and Aramaic Dictionary of the Old Testament, Greek Dictionary of the New Testament.* Nashville Tenn., T. Nelson, 1997.

The Expositor's Bible Commentary Luke – Acts
Tremper Longman, Iii, and David E Garland. *The Expositor's Bible Commentary Luke--Acts.* Grand Rapids, Mich., Zondervan, 2007.

Christ-Centered Exposition Series
Merida, Tony. Christ-Centered Exposition: Exalting Jesus in Acts. Nashville, TN, Holman Reference,, 2017.

The ESV Study Bible
Crossway Bibles. *ESV : Study Bible : English Standard Version.* Wheaton, Ill., Crossway Bibles, 2016.

Systematic Theology by Wayne Grudem
Grudem, Wayne A. *Systematic Theology.* Grand Rapids, Mich., Zondervan, 1994.

The Visual Word by Patrick Schreiner
Schreiner, Patrick, and Anthony M Benedetto. *The Visual Word : Illustrated Outlines of the New Testament Books.* Chicago, Moody Publishers, 2021.

The Gospel Coalition
"The Gospel Coalition." The Gospel Coalition, 18 Apr. 2019, www.thegospelcoalition.org.

ESV Story of Redemption Bible
Not Available. *HOLY BIBLE: English Standard Version, Story of Redemption Bible.* Crossway, 2018.

Pocket Dictionary of Theological Terms (Grenz, Guretzki + Nordling)
Grenz, Stanley J, et al. *Pocket Dictionary of Theological Terms.* Downers Grove, Ill., Intervarsity Press, 1999.

A discipleship community for working women who love Jesus.

If you've been looking for a community to come alongside you as you navigate the tension between what God's Word says and what culture wants us to believe, you belong here!

JOIN THE SWHW NETWORK:
SHEWORKSHISWAY.COM

We just know and believe in the power of gathering women together who want their work (inside & outside the home) to matter for the Kingdom of God. If you've been craving community, but don't know where to start – can we encourage you to start here? This simple step – choosing to invest in and equip yourself – can have an eternal impact on you, your people and your community. We'd love nothing more than to have you join the party!

THE SWHW PODCAST

You're invited into a conversation about how to navigate the tension between what God says and what culture wants you to believe, both Biblically and practically.

NEW EPISODE EVERY MONDAY

Scan code to connect with us

ADDITIONAL RESOURCES FROM SWHW:

  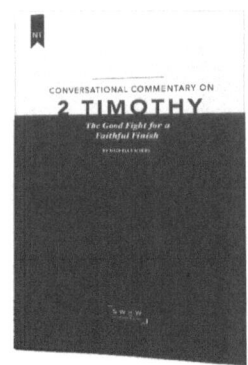

CONVERSATIONAL COMMENTARIES SERIES

SWHW BOOK + STUDY GUIDE, FAMOUS IN HEAVEN & AT HOME

100 DAILY DEVOTIONALS FOR THE WORKING WOMAN VOLS 1, 2, +3

SHEWORKSHISWAY.COM/SHOP

Become a
SHE WORKS HIS WAY
DONOR

100% of your gift helps us provide discipleship training for women and local churches around the world.

SHE WORKS HIS WAY is a registered 501(c)(3) non-profit organization.

SHEWORKSHISWAY.COM/DONATE

Made in United States
Troutdale, OR
07/11/2023